CONTENTS

 DRAWING 7

Monochrome Drawing Materials 14 Pencil 16
Charcoal 18 Conté Crayon 20 Pen & Ink 22 Line & Wash 24
Brush Drawing 26 Colour Drawing Materials 28 Coloured Pencil 30
Pastel Techniques 32 Inks & Markers 34 Comparative Demonstration 36
Making Accurate Drawings 38 Drawing Shapes 40 Drawing Form 42
Drawing with Line 44 Sketching 46 Figure Drawing 48
Pastel Demonstration 54 Animals 56 Coloured-pencil Demonstration 58
Buildings 60 Mixed-media Demonstration 64

 PASTEL PAINTING 69

About Pastels 70 Pastels 76 Papers 78 Line Strokes 80
Mixing Pastels 82 Exercise: Experimenting with Different Papers 86
Tinting your Paper 88 Underpainting 90 Wet Brushing Oil Pastel 92
Charcoal and Pastel 94 Building up Pastel 96
Laying a Textured Ground 98 Sgraffito 100
Comparative Demonstration 102 Landscape 106 Demonstration 110
Flowers 114 Demonstration 118 Faces & Figures 122

INDEX 126

Stockists & Suppliers 128

Drawing

Introduction
DRAWING

It is not easy to define the word "drawing" because it embraces a wide range of related but different activities. At its simplest it can be described as marks made on a sheet of paper, and in this sense it is one of the most basic of all human activities. Young children enjoy scribbling with a pencil or crayon as soon as they have developed sufficient manual dexterity to grip the implement, and long before they consider relating what they are doing to the world they see around them.

This enjoyment of the lines and marks made by various drawing implements is an important factor in all drawing, and para-mount in the work of some artists – the modern Swiss painter and draughtsman, Paul Klee, described his drawing as "taking a line for a walk". For most artists, however, drawing also performs a descriptive function: it is a direct response to the visual stimuli of our surroundings.

LEARNING TO DRAW
Drawing is often regarded as a special gift, and it is true that there are people who seem

TED GOULD
CLAIRE
(Above) *Pastel is a lovely medium for portraiture and is particularly well-suited to studies of children, as it creates gentle effects in keeping with the subject. On the face and clothing the artist has applied the colours lightly, rubbing them slightly into the paper to create soft blends, reinforced with crisp linear drawing.*

PIP CARPENTER
SWANS ON THE THAMES
(Left) *Pastel need not be a soft and delicate medium; it is extremely versatile and responsive to the artist's visual interests and ways of working. Here the artist has created energetic and exciting effects in the picture by laying heavy strokes of unblended colour, using the tip of the pastel stick.*

ROBERT
MAXWELL WOOD
YESTERDAY'S
NUDES, RADISHES
(Left) *In his picture, this
artist uses coloured
pencil in a completely
different way to John
Townend (below). He
achieves meticulous
detail and considerable
depth of colour with
successive layers of
coloured pencil, using
a delicate shading
technique so that almost
no lines are visible.*

to be able to draw quite effortlessly. Yet
drawing, like writing, is a skill which can be
acquired; if the motivation is there, most
people can learn to draw accurately. In the
past, students were taught to draw in a
certain way, with the emphasis on
mastering a specific set of techniques, but
this ignored the essential fact that drawing
is first and foremost about seeing.

TED GOULD
GIRL SKETCHING
(Right) *Wax crayon is a
less subtle drawing
medium than pastel, but
it has the advantage of
not smudging and is thus
useful for sketchbook
drawings and quick
impressions. In this
lively drawing, the artist
has built up the forms
and colours with a
network of loose
hatching and cross-
hatching lines.*

JOHN TOWNEND
SUMMER VIEW BEYOND THE POOL
(Above) *This artist works out of doors directly from
his subject, and finds coloured pencil ideal for his
particular approach. He uses the medium in a free and
instinctive manner, with bold hatching lines varying
in direction according to the forms he is describing.*

DAVID CUTHBERT
POLLY WANTS A POT
(Left) *In this delightful and inventive drawing,
coloured pencil has been pressed heavily into the
paper to achieve areas of heavy, almost flat colour.
The two-dimensional pattern element is stressed by
the use of coloured outlines.*

Although technical skill is important, it is not the first stage in learning how to draw, as it is pointless to develop techniques in a void. You may produce beautifully even lines of hatching and cross-hatching but still find that you have failed in the primary task of drawing, which is to describe the subject to your own satisfaction. Such failures are nearly always the direct result of poor observation, not of inadequate technique.

It sounds easy enough to say that if you want to learn how to draw all you need to do is to look at things, but it is not that simple, because you have to learn to look in a certain way, analytically and objectively. This can be a surprisingly hard skill to master, as it involves looking at a subject with a fresh eye every time, abandoning preconceptions. Our brains are cluttered with information which can be actively unhelpful in the context of drawing, leading us to quite the wrong conclusions – we tend to draw what we know from experience rather than what we see with our own eyes.

PAUL BARTLETT
STILL LIFE WITH
MAN-MADE AND
NATURAL OBJECTS
*A combination of pastel
and pastel pencil has
been used for this
exploration of shapes
and forms. The light
brown paper chosen by
the artist has allowed
him to build up both
highlights and shadows
with light overlays of
white and brown pastel.
It has also given a subtle
touch of colour to
what is essentially a
monochrome drawing.*

GERRY BAPTIST
BANANAS AND OTHER FRUIT
(Left) *This lovely drawing is also a study of form,
done in very soft pencil, which blunts easily and
thus provides broader, bolder effects than hard or
medium pencil. Both this and Bartlett's still life are
carefully composed, showing that a drawing in
monochrome can make as complete a statement
as a coloured drawing or painting.*

PAUL BARTLETT
SELF PORTRAIT
(Below) *A comparison between this drawing and
Gerry Baptist's demonstrates the versatility of the
pencil. Here the effect is almost photographic in its
minute attention to detail and texture and its subtle
gradations of tone.*

A classic example is relative size, which
can be hard to get right, particularly when
you are drawing familiar objects. If you
place one large object on a table with a
much smaller one in front of it, the chances
are that you will make the larger one too
large because of your prior knowledge of it.
But in fact the effects of perspective will
have caused it to "shrink", so that it may be
smaller than the object nearer to you. The
only way to approach drawing a known
subject, whether it be a portrait, an apple on

TED GOULD
GIRL IN AN ARMCHAIR
(Left) *Pen and ink can achieve intricate and elaborate
effects, but it is also a lovely medium for rapid line
drawings. In this figure study the artist has caught the
essentials of the pose in a few pen strokes, sometimes
superimposing lines where the first drawing was
incorrect or needed clarifying.*

JOHN TOWNEND
SHUNTING LOCOMOTIVE AT BOW
(Below) *For this sketch, made on location, the artist has used oil pastel, an ideal medium for bold effects and quick impressions, as colours can be built up rapidly. Also, unlike soft pastel, oil pastel does not smudge and does not require fixing. The sgraffito technique has been used to add touches of linear detail to the side of the coach.*

ELISABETH
HARDEN
NETTLES
(Above) *The attractive combination of pen lines and washes of diluted ink (watercolour can also be used) allows tones to be built up with greater speed than is possible with line alone. Pen and wash is ideal both for broad treatments and the kind of delicate effect seen in this drawing.*

a plate or a tree, is to force yourself to abandon preconceptions by pretending to yourself that you have never seen it before. Only in this way will you be able to assess it thoroughly and draw it accurately.

DIFFERENT KINDS OF DRAWING

A drawing can be many things: it can be a few lines of "visual shorthand" in a sketchbook, made to remind the artist of some salient point in a subject; it can be a first step in painting, subsequently hidden by layers of paint and thus having no independent existence; it can be a finished work of art in its own right, planned, composed and executed with as much thought as a painting.

PIP CARPENTER
THREE FISHES
(Right) *This is also a mixed-media work, but a more unusual combination has been used: oil paint, used thinly on paper, and coloured pencils. There are no set rules about mixed-media drawing; only by experimenting will you discover which work well together and which do not.*

The kind of drawing you make depends on how you view the purpose of the activity – why are you drawing? You may draw simply because you love to do so, in which case, once you have mastered the "alphabet" of drawing you will find it a satisfying means of self-expression. You may have aspirations to become an illustrator, or you may simply want to improve your observational skills because you enjoy painting.

If you view drawing as a necessary foundation skill for painting, accuracy will be the main aim, and it does not matter very much which medium you use, but for those who enjoy drawing for its own sake, it is rewarding to experiment with different media. There is now a wider choice of drawing materials than ever before, from the traditional graphite pencil to a whole range of colourful and versatile pastels, coloured pencils, inks and felt-tipped pens. The word "drawing" no longer conjures up an image of timid grey pencil marks on white paper – much more exciting effects than this are achievable.

JOAN ELLIOTT BATES
WHITE VILLAGE, SOUTH SPAIN
(Right) *In this delightful drawing – which could be described equally well as a painting – the artist has used pen and ink with light washes of watercolour. These have spread the ink in places so that there is no obvious boundary between line and colour. When using a mixture of media it is important that the two work together, or the drawing will lack unity.*

JOHN TOWNEND
EAST END FAMILY HOUSE
(Opposite) *In this pen-and-ink drawing, tones have been built up by hatching and cross-hatching, a method which can create a somewhat mechanical impression, but which has been used loosely here, with the lines almost scribbled over one another in varying directions. Pen and ink is a good medium for rapid location sketches like this, as the impossibility of erasing encourages a decisive approach.*

MONOCHROME DRAWING MATERIALS

Many people picture a drawing as a work in monochrome – pencil, pen and ink or charcoal. In the past most drawings were indeed in one colour or perhaps two, largely because colour drawing materials, with the exception of pastels, did not arrive on the art scene until relatively recently. Now there are a great many, which are discussed later. However, because most people begin drawing with monochrome materials we will look at these first.

PENCILS
These are the most basic of all drawing tools, as well as being one of the most sensitive and versatile. Few artists would be without a selection of pencils. Although they are sometimes incorrectly described as "lead", pencils are in fact made of graphite, a form of carbon, and began to be manufactured in the 18th century after the discovery of a deposit in the north of England. They are made in different grades, from 8B, which is very soft, to about 4H, which is much too hard for ordinary

WILLOW CHARCOAL

COMPRESSED CHARCOAL

CONTÉ CRAYONS

LARGE-SIZE
PENCIL

GRAPHITE STICK

PENCILS

drawing purposes. An HB, a 2B and a 4B would provide a good selection for the beginner to practise with.

CONTÉ CRAYONS
These are square-sectioned sticks, similar to hard pastels in consistency. They are made in black, white, and a selection of "earth" colours – browns and red-browns. They are capable of much bolder effects than pencil, and are excellent both for crisp, decisive lines and for areas of solid dark tone, as they can be sharpened to a point or broken into short lengths and used sideways. The

SHARPENERS

CARTRIDGE PAPER FIXED
TO DRAWING BOARD
WITH MASKING TAPE

ERASER

SCALPEL

only drawback is that Conté cannot be erased easily.

INTER-CHANGEABLE NIBS FOR PEN HOLDER

SELECTION OF DIP PENS

D R A W I N G

REED PEN

BAMBOO PEN

QUILL PEN

INK

SYNTHETIC BRUSHES

CHARCOAL

This is one of the most popular of all the monochrome media. Because it encourages a bold, uninhibited form of drawing, art teachers often recommend it to novices. Charcoal is made from fired twigs of wood, such as willow, and is sold in different thicknesses. It smudges easily, and corrections can be made simply by wiping it off; however, this makes it less suitable than pencil for small-scale sketchbook work.

Compressed charcoal is also available, in both stick and pencil form. This produces deeper, richer blacks than ordinary charcoal, but is less easy to erase.

PENS, INKS AND BRUSHES

There are a great many different kinds of pen, ranging from modern felt- and fibre-tips to "old-fashioned" implements such as quills and reed pens. Perhaps it is best to start with one of the inexpensive wooden or plastic handles sold with a set of various interchangeable nibs which will enable you to practise your "handwriting" in pen and ink; this type of pen may well remain a favourite item of equipment, as it does for many professional artists.

There is a variety of drawing inks on the market, but they can be divided into two basic types: water-soluble and waterproof, the latter being shellac- or acrylic-based. Water-soluble ink can be diluted with water and is therefore useful for wash drawings, where you want a range of greys as well as black. Waterproof ink should never be used in reservoir-type pens, as it clogs them up. Felt- and fibre-tipped pens are also made in waterproof and water-soluble versions – check in your art shop, as they are not always clearly labelled. Brushes are not a necessity, but they are sensitive drawing implements, producing an expressive line.

PAPERS

The most common surface for drawing is plain white cartridge (drawing) paper. For wash drawings, make sure that you buy good-quality cartridge (drawing) paper.

Some artists prefer to use a paper with a texture for charcoal drawings. Textured paper can also be used for Conté drawings. If you want solid blacks (or browns), however, stick to smooth cartridge (drawing) paper.

ADDITIONAL EQUIPMENT

A rigid board of some kind is required to support the paper. You will also need erasers, a craft knife and a can of spray fixative if you intend to use charcoal.

SPRAY FIXATIVE

LIQUID FIXATIVE

MOUTH DIFFUSER

BLACK INKS

PENCIL

As the pencil is such a versatile drawing implement, it allows each artist to develop his or her own "handwriting" in drawing. There are so many different ways of using pencil that no one technique or set of techniques can really be singled out as belonging particularly to this medium.

LINE AND TONE

The grade of pencil and the subject you choose to draw are both major influences on the way you use the pencil. An HB pencil, for example, gives light, fine lines, so it is not suitable for broad effects involving heavy shading and smudging methods. This relatively hard pencil would be a good choice for a subject such as flowers, where fine lines and delicate areas of tone could be built up by light shading or hatching and cross-hatching. The latter technique, which is used in all the line media, is dealt with in more detail under pen and ink.

Soft pencils, such as 6B and 8B, can create thick dark areas; indeed a drawing in soft pencil can look very similar to one in Conté crayon. These pencils are most suitable for drawings in which line plays a subsidiary role. They are ideal for rendering tonal effects, such as light and shade in a landscape or the modelling on forms – perhaps a face or figure seen in strong side-lighting. If you are drawing or sketching out of doors, rather than working from a subject that you have set up specially at home, take a good selection of pencils with you, as your initial direct response to the subject will often dictate the kind of drawing that you make.

PENCILS

Marks made with a 2B pencil   *Marks made with a 4B pencil*   *Marks made with an 8B pencil*

FROTTAGE

This is a specialist technique which is worth knowing about. It is not restricted to pencil drawing – charcoal, Conté crayon or pastel can also be used. The term "frottage" comes from the French verb *frotter*, to rub, and the method will be familiar to anyone who has made or seen brass rubbings. A piece of paper is placed over a textured surface, or one with an incised pattern, and soft pencil is rubbed over the paper. The method is often used to create areas of pattern or texture in a drawing – for example, patterns of wood grain taken from a rough piece of timber could be incorporated into a still life. The effects which can be achieved vary according to the paper used. Brass rubbings are done on thin paper because this yields the crispest and clearest impressions; on ordinary drawing paper, pencil frottage produces a more blurred result which may suggest a texture without being specific as to its nature.

Frottage method

You need a soft pencil and fairly thin paper for a clear impression. Here a graphite stick (a pencil without the wooden casing) is used to take a rubbing from a piece of bubble wrap.

6 (Right) The finished collage shows an interesting use of frottage, which can be difficult to use in a "normal" drawing.

Collage of frottage textures

1 A variety of frottage textures has been obtained from surfaces in the artist's home. These have been made on thin cartridge (drawing) paper, which has given good impressions; it is also easier to stick down than thick paper.

2 A working drawing is made first to plan the composition, with light shading indicating where the dark and light tones are to be placed.

3 A tracing has been made from the drawing, and lines are transferred to the back of each piece of paper. The first piece is cut out.

4 The artist moves the collage pieces around for the best placing before gluing them down in their final positions.

5 At a certain point, she begins to depart from the shapes in the master drawing, letting the collage develop independently.

CHARCOAL

Charcoal is a wonderfully versatile medium, responsive to the slightest change in the amount of pressure applied, depending on how the stick is held. Fine sticks of willow charcoal can produce either delicate effects or tough, crisp lines resembling those in certain pencil drawings, while at the other extreme, a thick stick of charcoal or compressed charcoal used on its side allows you to build up deep, rich areas of tone.

Ordinary cartridge (drawing) paper has a smooth surface, which does not hold the charcoal well, so for drawings where tone is more important than line, you may need either to spray the work with fixative at intervals or to use a paper with more texture, such as Ingres paper, watercolour paper or recycled paper. These will grip the charcoal dust more firmly and allow you to achieve a denser coverage. For line drawings or fine, light effects, however, cartridge (drawing) paper is ideal.

ERASING TECHNIQUES

Charcoal can be erased completely, but this is somewhat laborious and not in keeping with the boldness and immediacy of the medium; it is more usual to rub down any incorrect lines, producing an area of grey with "ghost lines" which can be drawn over. These, which are often an exciting feature of drawings in charcoal, are helpful from a practical point of view too, as it is easier to correct or amend a drawing when the wrong lines are still visible.

The ease with which charcoal can be rubbed down has given rise to an interesting technique known as "lifting out". This

WILLOW CHARCOAL

Charcoal on Ingres paper

Charcoal on watercolour paper

Lifting out charcoal

1 *Having covered a sheet of cartridge (drawing) paper with charcoal, the artist wipes it down with cotton wool (a cotton ball) to produce grey.*

2 *A rough drawing over the grey background establishes the darker tones of the picture and provides a guide for the highlights to be lifted out.*

3 *Using a putty eraser, the artist works on the main light areas of the subject, using the side of the eraser for broad strokes and the corner for finer detail.*

4 *The darker areas have been defined with further bold applications of charcoal, and the corner of the eraser is now used to create a new highlight.*

5 *For the finer details, the putty eraser is pulled into a point and used as one might use a pastel stick or pencil.*

6 *(Right) The method encourages bold drawing and dramatic, painterly effects – the lifted-out highlights look similar to brushstrokes.*

reverses the usual drawing procedure, in which the darkest tones are built up gradually; here you work from dark to light, picking out the highlights with a putty eraser. This method is often applied to figure drawing – art teachers find it encourages an unfussy approach – but any subject which has strong contrasts of tone can be drawn in this way.

The usual method is to start by covering the whole of the paper with charcoal, rub it down to produce an overall mid-grey and then make a line drawing over this. The drawing is in turn rubbed down to produce a ghost image which provides a guide for the next stage – that of lifting out the highlights. Once the main highlights are in place, the mid-tones are established by working more lightly with the eraser, after which the darks can be strengthened if necessary with further applications of charcoal. It is not as difficult as it sounds, and you can achieve quite precise effects with the putty eraser, which can be pulled into a point for fine lines and used on the flat for large areas.

CONTÉ CRAYON

Conté crayon on cartridge (drawing) paper

Black Conté crayons and Conté pencils give a less subtle line than charcoal or pencil, but are excellent for bold effects. Conté crayons are made from natural earth pigments held together with a binder, which makes them less crumbly than charcoal, enabling you to build up solid areas of black because the colour grips the paper more firmly. You don't usually need to fix Conté drawings, as they don't smudge easily, but it is difficult to erase mistakes cleanly. The brown and brownish-red crayons and pencils yield more delicate effects and are perhaps more sympathetic to use than the black – throughout the history of art the so-called "sanguine" (red-brown) chalks or crayons have been much favoured for portrait and figure drawings.

PAPER TEXTURE

As with charcoal drawings, the texture of the paper plays a part in the final appearance of the work, but here the smoother the paper, the darker the drawing will be. A textured surface, such as pastel paper or medium-surface watercolour paper, breaks up the strokes, allowing tiny specks of white to show through to create a slight speckling which can be highly effective in a light- or mid-toned drawing.

Conté crayon on Ingres paper

Conté crayon on watercolour paper

WORKING À TROIS COULEURS

Drawings in sanguine Conté crayons are often done on a lightly coloured paper, usually a warm cream or light brown, which enhances the rich colours. For a low-key effect, black Conté can be used on a grey or blue paper, which provides a middle tone. Such drawings can be left as they are, with only dark and mid-tones, but a traditional technique is to pick out the highlights in white Conté, using, in effect, three colours – hence *trois couleurs*. This is an excellent way to model form, and the method was extensively used by the old masters for nude studies. Areas of the paper are left uncovered, while the light and dark tones are achieved by shading with white and black (or sanguine and brown) Conté respectively. Very subtle and beautiful effects can be achieved in this way.

1 *The artist is working on off-white Ingres paper, and has begun the drawing in dark brown Conté crayon. She uses black to strengthen some lines slightly.*

2 *A middle tone has been established with loose diagonal hatching lines of sanguine crayon; black is again used lightly on the shadowed side of the face and neck.*

3 *The face is now beginning to take on solid, three-dimensional form, although the crayon work is still light and delicate.*

4 *Highlights have been added in white crayon, and the whole face comes alive with the definition of the eyes.*

5 *A putty eraser is used to soften the patch of dark shading at the corner of the mouth. Conté cannot be erased completely, but it can be softened and smudged.*

6 (Right) *The finished drawing has the look of a painting, although only three colours have been used, plus white and the colour of the paper.*

The pencil was a relatively recent arrival on the art scene, but pen and ink have been with us for many centuries; in China, inks were being made as early as 2,550 BC, and in Ancient Egypt reed pens were used for both writing and drawing. Reed pens, bamboo pens and quill pens – the latter being the standard writing implement in Europe until the 19th century – are now enjoying a major artistic revival, and are well worth experimenting with. They can be bought from specialist suppliers or you can make your own, as many artists do.

However, there are also many different types of ready-made pen on the market today, all of which create different effects.

SCRIBBLE DRAWING

You can also build up tones and forms in a looser, less-organized way, by scribbling with the pen. This is a harder technique to handle than hatching and cross-hatching as it has a random quality – you must learn to let the pen do the work, moving around freely until the correct density is built up. It was a technique much used by Picasso when in revolt against traditional methods, and can give a dynamic quality to a drawing.

1 *A fine fibre-tipped pen has been used for this self-portrait, and the forms have been constructed in a free and spontaneous way, with the pen moving almost randomly over the paper.*

2 *Here the same technique has been used for an animal drawing. In this case the artist worked from a photograph because scribble drawing takes longer than a line sketch in pencil or charcoal, and is thus not ideal for a live, moving subject.*

HATCHING AND CROSS-HATCHING

As pen and ink is uncompromising in its linearity – you can't shade and smudge as you can with pencil and charcoal – tones must be described with a network of lines. Hatching lines are those which go in one direction, while in cross-hatching a further set of lines is made on top of those in the opposite direction. Obviously the closer together the lines are, the darker the tone will be.

These methods offer numerous possibilities, because, although the lines should be roughly parallel, they need not be straight and even. The traditional method of hatching was to use a series of slanting lines, and this is still the commonest technique, but the lines can curve slightly to follow the shape of certain objects. This can give a less-mechanical look to the finished drawing, and also helps to build up a three-dimensional impression.

1 The artist is using a fine, metal-pointed pen of the kind used by graphic designers, and is working on a sheet of good-quality cartridge (drawing) paper.

2 She will introduce more of the drapery at a later stage, but she begins with the pears on the plate. Notice how she has varied the hatching lines, from long diagonals to small dots and dashes.

3 The forms of the pears are built up more solidly with further hatching lines, which are denser and closer together at the centre of the pear, where there is an area of dark shadow.

4 With pears and plate complete, further work is then carried out on the drapery, with lightly scribbled lines deepening the shadow in the foreground.

5 (Right) The drawing is a convincing rendering of three-dimensional form, and the variety of different lines creates a lively effect. Although all roughly diagonal, they are only parallel and evenly spaced where the artist wanted to describe the flat plane of the table top.

You really need to try them out to discover which ones you prefer, but fortunately most good art shops will let you do this, and provide pads of paper for scribbling on.

To some extent your choice will depend on the kind of drawing you intend to do and where you are working. For example, a fibre- or felt-tipped pen would be unlikely to provide the delicacy of line needed for a flower study, but might be ideal for quick outdoor sketches in the town or countryside, as a bottle of ink is not required. Don't neglect the possibilities of the humble ballpoint pen either – this can be a useful drawing tool, with the added advantage of being familiar to handle.

LINE & WASH

Another way to build up areas of tone in a pen-and-ink drawing is to combine the line element with washes made from diluted water-soluble ink or black watercolour. This method is used in watercolour painting, when the washes are in colour, but it is equally effective for introducing tone to monochrome drawings.

It is an attractive and enjoyable technique, allowing you to work more freely and rapidly than you can with pen alone, because you don't have to rely on the line to provide the tone. Both Rembrandt and Nicolas Poussin in the 17th century exploited line and wash with consummate skill, producing beautifully expressive drawings. The technique is closely associated with figure drawing, but it is equally suitable for other subjects, such as landscapes, urban scenes and flowers.

PENS AND PAPERS

A varied line gives the best effect, so this might be the time to try out quill, bamboo or reed pens. You can use drawing pens or felt-tips, but these tend to create a slightly rigid impression because the line is always the same thickness. Interesting effects can be created by working with a bamboo pen on a slightly textured watercolour paper, rather than cartridge (drawing) paper, as this produces a "dry", broken line.

If you intend to use a good deal of wash you may need to stretch the paper first, otherwise it could buckle under the water and spoil your work. Soak the paper in a bath for a few minutes, lift it out carefully and shake off the excess water, then place it on a drawing board and stick gumstrip (gummed brown paper tape) all around the edges, smoothing the paper with a damp sponge as you work. Leave it to dry naturally if possible; if you put it in front of

Using brush and reed pens

1 *This subject has contrasting areas of light and shadow, so the artist begins by working in tone, using a large soft brush and water-soluble ink.*

2 *A reed pen is used, with undiluted ink, to draw into the washes. These pens give a bolder but more sensitive line than mechanically produced drawing pens.*

3 *Line is not intended to play a dominant role, so pen and brush-work are developed at the same time, with darker washes now painted over the pen lines.*

4 *The drawing is at a halfway stage, and the artist assesses it to see which areas require further definition. Notice that, because water-soluble ink has been used, the washes of diluted ink have spread and softened the pen lines.*

5 *The shadow on the left-hand building has been deepened with further washes, and the reed pen is used again, this time with well-watered ink, to make light lines at the top of the steps.*

the fire or use a hairdryer, the tape will dry before the paper and may tear off.

WORKING METHODS

In order to produce a well-integrated drawing, try to develop the line and wash together, rather than "filling in" a line drawing. One way to do this is to use water-soluble ink in the pen, as you can spread this with a brush and clean water in places to soften the line and then apply more washes as required. However, some artists prefer the line to remain crisp; they use waterproof ink in the pen and water-soluble ink for the washes. You can also reverse the normal procedure (which is to begin with the drawing) and lay some washes first in order to establish the tonal structure of the subject, using pen later to add details and touches of definition. This could be a particularly suitable approach for a landscape subject.

6 The steps play an important part in the composition, as they lead the eye in towards the focal point, which is the church tower, so they are defined carefully with a combination of washes and decisive pen work.

7 The bold, broad lines of the reed pen complement the loose washes to create a well-integrated drawing. At the bottom of the wall on the left, the artist has exploited one of the semi-accidental effects known as backruns, which quite often occur in wash and watercolour work, to suggest the texture of old plasterwork.

BRUSH DRAWING

In a pen-and-wash drawing, the pen provides the linear element; you can, however, dispense with the pen altogether and make drawings entirely with a brush, a method which takes you into the area of painting. The tip of a good brush can provide quite fine definition and, if this is combined with washes, the effect is similar to that of a pen-and-wash drawing but softer, and the line and tone are automatically well-integrated because the same implement has been used for both. Rembrandt made some wonderful brush-and-wash figure drawings, and the great 19th-century English landscape painter, John Constable, used the method for landscape sketches – it is particularly well suited to quick on-the-spot tonal studies.

A variant on the method is to work on dampened paper, which spreads and diffuses the washes to create soft effects, ideal for subjects such as misty landscapes and certain weather conditions. The paper must be stretched first, as explained on the preceding pages. Until you have practised the method it can be tricky to control the flow and spread of the ink, so begin with the larger areas of light washes and save the more detailed work done with the point of the brush until the later stages, when the paper has begun to dry or dried completely.

Ink and wash

1 *Having laid some light washes of watered ink, the artist works into them before they have dried so that the darker ink spreads and diffuses softly.*

2 *Still working wet into wet, she uses a piece of kitchen paper to control the flow of the ink. In the foreground, the washes have formed blobs with irregular edges, an effect she likes and therefore makes no attempt to correct.*

3 *The original ink washes on the trees have dried out to some extent, and the undiluted black ink now introduced hardly spreads at all. The artist is using a Chinese brush, which is ideal for this kind of drawing.*

4 *For the final stages a crisp effect was needed, so the paper was left to dry before further work was done on the background, the foreground wall and now the trees.*

5 *(Right) The brush-and-wash method allows you to build up an impression of the landscape more rapidly than is possible with a pencil or pen. The finished picture also provides a good example of the way accidental effects can enhance a drawing or painting; the backruns in the foreground provide a touch of interest and echo the shapes of the trees.*

Brush and paint

(Above and right) *In these studies, brush drawing has been taken a step further towards painting, with a combination of ink and watercolour used.*

Brush and ink

Both these drawings were done in no more than ten minutes, with slightly diluted brown ink and a Chinese brush. The method is excellent for quick figure drawings and studies of movement.

THE BRUSH AS LINE

Another kind of brush drawing is that done with line alone, using the brush purely as a drawing tool. This also takes practice, and is slightly unnerving initially because you cannot correct errors; nevertheless it is an exciting method to try, and you may find that it releases some inhibitions and makes your drawing freer and less fussy. You can do almost anything with a brush, depending on the type you use, how you hold it and the amount of pressure you apply, so it is worth making some "doodles" to explore the possibilities. The Oriental artists and calligraphers, who have exploited the potential of brush drawing for centuries, have evolved many different hand positions; sometimes they work with the brush vertical and held loosely near the top of the handle rather than gripped firmly at the ferrule.

COLOUR DRAWING MATERIALS

Drawing with pencils, charcoal and pens provides valuable practice and can be highly satisfying too, but with the coloured drawing media you can really experiment and produce works which are as expressive and as polished as any painting. Today's artists are in the fortunate position of having a wide range of high-quality materials to choose from – the only problem being where to start.

COLOURED PENCILS

These make a good starting point for anyone launching into colour; they are easy to use, handling in the same way as the familiar graphite pencil, and you can start with a few colours and built up a more extensive collection gradually.

Like all colour media they are made from pigment held together with a binder. The quantity of binder used varies from one manufacturer to another, so you will find

OIL PASTELS

HARD PASTELS

differences in consistency between brands. Some pencils are soft, chalky and opaque, resembling pastels; some are slightly greasy, and others are hard and fairly transparent. You will only discover which ones you like by trying them out, which is one very good reason for starting with a small range.

SOFT PASTELS

COLOURED PENCILS

Some manufacturers make water-soluble pencils as well, which are particularly useful because you can use them both wet and dry, spreading the colour in some parts of a drawing and using lines in others.

PASTELS

Pastels are made in soft and hard versions, with the former, sold in the form of cylindrical sticks, being favoured by "pastel painters". These are almost pure pigment, bound with a tiny amount of gum, and are consequently very crumbly. Hard pastels, made with a higher proportion of binder, come in square-sectioned sticks. They produce much crisper, clearer lines and do not smudge as easily. Pastel pencils are also good for linear effects – they are somewhere in between hard and soft pastels in their consistency. Spray fixative is necessary for any drawings in pastel.

Oil pastels have the great advantage of not requiring fixative, as the pigment is bound with waxes and oils. The variation in consistency from range to range is enormous, with some pastels being quite hard and others almost melting in your hand, but there are two basic categories: wax-oil pastels and non-wax ones, simply called oil pastels. The former have their devotees, but in general they are less malleable than standard oil pastels, which are a versatile and fluent drawing medium.

INKS AND MARKERS

Coloured drawing inks, like black inks, can be divided into two broad types: waterproof and water-soluble. They are made in a wide range of brilliant colours and can be mixed together to increase the range further. Some waterproof inks are bound with shellac, which means they can't be mixed successfully with water-based inks, but others are acrylic-based – they are known as liquid acrylics and they behave in use very much like water-soluble inks, except that they are impermeable when dry.

If you want your work to last, guard against the type of ink called "brilliant watercolour"; this is made not from pigment but from dyes, which can fade and discolour. The colours are temptingly vivid, but they are made for graphic reproduction work, where the discoloration of the original may not matter.

Some coloured felt-tipped pens are also prone to fading and should be checked carefully before buying. These pens are made either with broad wedge-shaped tips (these are sometimes called markers) or with fine tips, and the ink used in them can be water- or spirit-based. They are ideal for those who like a bold approach to drawing.

PAPERS

For coloured-pencil and oil-pastel work, and ink drawing, good-quality cartridge (drawing) paper can be used, though some artists who specialize in coloured pencil or oil pastel like to use a rougher texture and sometimes a pre-coloured paper. For chalk-pastel work, smooth paper is not usually suitable, as the pigment tends to fall off, so it is best to use either one of the papers made specially for pastel work – Ingres or Mi-Teintes paper – or watercolour paper. If you like the texture of the latter but prefer to work on coloured paper, you can tint it with a light wash of water-colour first.

MARKERS

COLOURED INKS

COLOURED PENCIL

Although coloured pencils are becoming increasingly popular with fine artists, both for sketching and for finished works, at one time they were mainly associated with illustration work, and are still widely used for this purpose. In order to accommodate commercial demands, manufacturers produce coloured pencils in a wide range of hues and shades – some offer as many as two hundred. However, as colours can be mixed on the picture surface, it is not necessary to buy a complete range and, even if you did, you would still have to rely on mixing to some extent, particularly for dark colours, which can only be achieved by building up in layers.

COLOUR MIXING

Colours can be mixed in a number of different ways, the classic method being hatching and crosshatching, explained under pen and ink drawing. This method allows you to achieve subtle colour mixing effects as well as considerable depth of colour. Blues lightly hatched over yellow and then crosshatched in places with deeper blues will produce beautifully varied areas of green, while colour could be introduced into shadow areas by hatching and crosshatching over black with dark blues and purples.

While this is a good method for highly finished, detailed work, it is not a rapid process, added to which too many tight layers of hatching and crosshatching can make a drawing appear overworked and lacking in spontaneity. For a looser effect, tones can be built up simply by shading, the method you would naturally use with an ordinary graphite pencil. Colours can also be mixed in this way, with yellow shaded over red producing orange, and yellow over blue making green, for example.

Colours and tones can be built up by careful shading.

Colours are often mixed by hatching and cross-hatching.

The tip of a water-soluble pencil has been dipped in water before laying the colour over the blue.

Both pencils have been dipped in water, and a wet brush taken over the whole area to produce this effect.

Burnishing

1 *The colours must be built up solidly in the part of the drawing to be burnished. Here a white pencil is used to burnish highlights.*

2 *An eraser removes a little of the pigment, but also pushes the remaining particles into one another, creating soft blends.*

3 *As you can see in the finished picture, white pencil modifies the colour beneath, and therefore works better on highlight areas. For burnishing dark colours a torchon is more effective.*

With water-soluble pencils the colour-mixing possibilities are increased; you can spread colour into a wash with water and a clean brush, overlay this with another colour, mix the second colour into the first with more water, and so on. However, don't overdo mixing wet washes of colours, as some of the coloured pencil pigments have a chalky quality and leave a muddy, colourless mess when mixed wet.

1 *If you are uncertain of the design you can work it out first on ordinary paper and then trace it, but in this case the artist draws directly onto the tracing paper.*

2 *She places the tracing paper over the working surface and, before starting the impressing, fixes it at the top with a piece of masking tape to prevent slippage.*

BURNISHING

This method can be used to increase the brilliance of colours in certain areas of a drawing, but it is not suitable for water-soluble pencils used wet. Having been built up thickly, the colours are then rubbed with a plastic eraser or torchon (a rolled paper stump sold for blending pastels). This action pushes the particles of pigment into one another so that no separate lines or marks are visible; the grain of the paper is flattened to produce a sheen.

IMPRESSING

If you draw with coloured pencil on a heavily textured paper, most of the pigment will be deposited on the top of the weave; impressing follows the same principle. "Blind" lines are pressed into the paper with a knitting needle or paintbrush handle and, when coloured pencil is applied on top, the lines show as white. The method is also known as white line drawing.

You can use impressed lines simply for variety in a drawing, but quite intricate pattern effects are possible too. If the white line is to play a major role in the drawing it is helpful to use tracing paper to place the lines accurately. Draw up your design, trace it – or draw it directly onto tracing paper – then lay the tracing on your drawing paper and go over the lines with a hard pencil.

3 *She goes over all the lines with a hard pencil. You can use any pointed implement for this, but a pencil is the best choice for a complex design, as you can keep track of which lines you have drawn over.*

4 *The lines show up clearly through the coloured pencil, which is applied quite heavily. The working surface is smooth watercolour paper which, being thicker than cartridge (drawing) paper, produces more positive indentations.*

5 *With several reds and orange-reds shaded over one another, black is now used lightly to give greater depth of colour, contrasting with the white lines.*

PASTEL TECHNIQUES

D
R
A
W
I
N
G

There is always argument about whether a work in pastel should be classified as a drawing or a painting, but this merely underlines the fact that there is no real boundary between the two. In general, a pastel with an obvious linear emphasis is considered to be a drawing while those in which colours are built up thickly in layering techniques and line plays a minor role, are clearly paintings, although not done with a brush.

PASTEL MARKS

In the context of drawing, it is the mark-making capacity of pastels rather than their ability to build up colours that is most important, and in this field they are supreme among the media. A coloured pencil can only produce lines and, although these can be thick, thin, heavy or light, there are few other possible permutations. Pastels, whether you use the hard or soft variety, have a far greater inherent range: they can be sharpened to a point to produce crisp, incisive marks, used blunt for softer lines, or broken into short lengths and used sideways to make strokes of colour.

Pastel pencils are less versatile in mark-making terms, handling very much like coloured pencils except that they are considerably softer. They are also softer than hard pastels and cannot produce the same fine lines that are possible with the edge of a square-sectioned hard pastel stick. However, they are pleasant to use, and excellent for relatively small-scale work. The colour can be partially spread with water and a clean brush to produce a wash effect and to soften lines where necessary.

OIL PASTELS

Oil pastels don't make very crisp lines either, but they are ideal for bold drawings

SOFT PASTEL

HARD PASTEL

OIL PASTEL

PASTEL PENCILS

and vivid, solid areas of colour. Some artists prefer them to soft pastels, as they are less crumbly, less fragile and do not require fixing. Furthermore, they allow you to make use of a technique called sgraffito, in which one layer of colour is scratched back to reveal another. A variety of effects can be achieved in this way, from fine lines made with a sharp implement to more subtle broken-colour effects, achieved by scraping back successive layers of colour with the edge of a knife.

PAPERS

The quality of the lines and marks you make with pastels, whichever kind you use,

1 *Working on a smooth-surfaced watercolour paper, the artist lays the colours thickly, making sure that the oily pastel is pushed well into the paper.*

2 *Some areas of these first colours will be overlaid with darker ones, but selected parts will be either left uncovered or revealed by scratching, so the artist has chosen them with the finished effect in mind.*

3 *With dark green now laid thickly on top of the yellow, the point of a knife is used to scratch fine lines. This has also removed a little of the original colour, but the lines are not white because the pigment has stained the paper.*

4 *The sgraffito effect has been built up all over the leaves, with varying pressure of the knife. Here it is used quite lightly.*

is considerably affected by the paper you work on. For a pastel painting, where you intend to build up colours thickly, it is usual to work on textured paper, as smooth paper does not grip the pigment sufficiently firmly. This reduces the solidity of the line, breaking up the stroke slightly so that some of the paper shows through. For purely line work, where you don't intend to lay one colour over another, you can use smoother paper, which gives a solid, unbroken line without the paper showing through. You might also try one of the special papers sold for pastel work – velour paper. This provides a line which is both solid and soft, with slightly fuzzy edges.

5 *Although you can scratch into light colours to reveal dark ones in exactly the same way, the technique is most effective when worked dark to light, as in this drawing.*

INKS & MARKERS

The idea of drawing with a brush can be taken a step further by using several different colours of drawing inks. These can be painted on straight from the bottle, mixed to produce a wide range of colours, or diluted with water (if you use water-based or acrylic-based inks) to form light washes of colour. In this way you can produce anything from a drawing made with several bold brushstrokes to something which closely resembles a painting in watercolour.

Coloured inks can be combined with black inks, applied either with a brush or a pen, or used in mixed-media techniques with other painting or drawing media such as acrylic paints, charcoal or oil pastels.

DRAWING WITH MARKERS

Markers and coloured felt-tipped pens are exciting to draw with, but because they are not capable of subtle effects, they are more suitable for sketches and quick impressions. Both markers (the chunky implements with broad wedge-shaped "nibs") and felt-tips are basically reservoir pens containing ink, which may be either spirit- or water-based. Water-based inks are better for sketching than spirit-based ones which tend to "bleed" into the paper so that some of the colour comes through onto the other side. The inks are transparent, so colours can be mixed on the paper surface by laying one over another; they can also be used in conjunction with drawing inks.

Markers on textured paper

Used on smooth paper, markers create a solid, uncompromising line, but here the texture of the watercolour paper has broken up the strokes to produce a lighter effect.

(Right, above and below) *Markers appeal to those who enjoy a bold approach, as they are not capable of subtle effects. They are, however, well suited to quick sketches such as these.*

Drawing with coloured inks

1 *You can make a light pencil drawing as a guide for pen lines if you wish, but in this case the artist begins in inks straightaway.*

2 *The purple flowers, and some lightly drawn red ones behind them, have provided a key for judging the other colours, and the artist now describes the shape of the patch of grass by making dark blue pen marks over green.*

3 *She is using a selection of different pens and has swapped the original broad-nibbed pen for a finer one in order to vary the quality of the lines.*

4 *The broad-nibbed pen is used again, as this area of the picture needs bold effects. Even with just one pen, the marks can be varied according to how it is held – notice how in the small plant on the left, the line changes from thick to thin.*

WAX RESIST

One of the best-known of the mixed-media drawing methods is wax resist, which is based on the incompatibility of oil and water. A drawing is made with wax crayons, wax oil pastels, an oil bar (oil paint in solid form) or an ordinary household candle, then water-based inks are laid on top; the wax subsequently repels the ink, creating a variety of fascinating effects.

5 *The background and right-hand area of foreground have been left until last, as the artist wanted to establish the central area before deciding how to treat the other parts of the picture. The contrast between the fine lines used for the background and the bolder drawing of the foreground and middleground helps to create a sense of space as well as adding interest to the drawing.*

COMPARATIVE DEMONSTRATION

D
R
A
W
I
N
G

There is a wide range of colour drawing media on the market today, and you may need to experiment with several in order to discover which one suits your own style and pictorial interests which can be expensive. However, you can learn a lot by looking at and responding to other artists' work. For example, you may like the effects you see in coloured pencil drawings better than those achieved by pastel or oil pastel, in which case you would do well to follow this initial response. Here two artists demonstrate two

very different media in order to show how the medium affects your way of working. Elizabeth Moore creates subtle effects with coloured pencil, while Judy Martin has chosen oil pastel, a much bolder medium capable of strong, vivid colours.

Coloured pencil on cartridge (drawing) paper

1 *When there is any build-up of coloured pencil it cannot be erased, so the artist begins by working very lightly, making sure that the skull is correctly drawn before she continues.*

2 *Having established the overall colour of the skull, laying one colour over another in places, she now works on the shadow, which plays an important part in the composition of the drawing.*

Oil pastel on coloured paper

1 *With a very light pencil drawing as a guide, the artist has begun with patches of white, dark browns and greys. Excited by the reflected colours on the skull, she works on these at an early stage.*

2 *The darkest and brightest areas of the picture have now been established – the vivid red background and one of the animal's horns. The red was particularly important because it would be difficult to assess the colours needed for the skull without some of this colour in place.*

3 In any line medium, whether pencil, coloured pencil or pastel, it is important to vary the marks you make, and here you can see a wide range, from long hatching lines on the table top to shorter, curving strokes describing the forms of the skull.

4 Here again, over earlier light hatching, the artist has applied short jabs, squiggles and curving lines that follow the direction of the forms. Notice also the variety of colours describing the skull, and the subtle mixtures produced by laying one colour over another.

5 If you compare the finished drawing with the oil-pastel one, you will see the extent to which the medium dictates the treatment of the subject. Because it is difficult to cover large areas with coloured pencil, the artist has only suggested the red paper, making the skull the most colourful part of the painting.

3 As in the coloured pencil drawing, the shadow plays an important part in the picture. Although the arrangement is the same in both cases, the lighting was altered to produce a longer, more angular shadow.

4 The colours of the skull are now intensified. Because she is working on coloured paper, the artist uses white pastel for the highlights rather than "reserving" them as she would on white paper.

5 Oil pastel is a much bolder medium than coloured pencil and, being soft, it covers large areas relatively quickly. These qualities have allowed the artist to exploit the dramatic red, black and white colour theme of the subject.

MAKING ACCURATE DRAWINGS

Having looked at the different drawing media and seen the various effects they can achieve, the next step is to learn how to use them to make a drawing that describes your subject with the required degree of accuracy so that it looks 'real'. Accurate drawing should in no way be confused with detailed drawing – a few lines can provide a better likeness of a subject, whether it be a face, a figure or a landscape, than any amount of careful detail. It is largely a matter of getting the shape, the proportion and the relative scale of an object right, and this requires first and foremost careful observation and constant checking.

Learning to draw is like learning to write – the basic skills must be mastered before you can make them work for you. It is easy to be put off by early failures in drawing and to decide you simply haven't got "the gift", but you can minimize such failures by following some simple strategies, at least when you first start to draw.

DRAWING SIGHT SIZE

Most artists use some system of measuring when they draw, and this is easiest if you draw the size you see. The term "sight size" is self-explanatory, and many people draw in this way naturally. Others don't – they tend to try to draw as near as possible to life size, and have to force themselves to reduce their drawings.

You can check very easily what sight-size is by placing an object such as a mug on a table and holding up a sketchbook in front of it, in the position from which you might draw it. Then close one eye and make two marks on the paper, one for each side of the mug. If you are outdoors drawing a landscape or an urban scene you can make a series of these "placement marks" across the top of your paper. This can be done

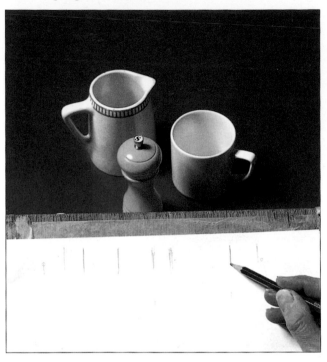

1 *With one eye closed, the artist begins by making a series of marks across the top of the paper so that he can establish the horizontal measurements. When drawing a small still-life group of this kind, you need to be quite close to the subject.*

either by holding up a pencil at the same level as your drawing and moving your thumb up and down it, or by using a ruler and reading the measurements.

It may seem a mechanical way of drawing, but when accuracy is required it is very helpful. If you are making an under-drawing for a painting, for example, rather than just drawing for its own sake, accuracy is more important than expressive qualities, and you will avoid having to make corrections when you paint.

MEASURING BY COMPARISON

Drawing sight-size is easier than trying to scale objects up or down in your mind, but it doesn't always work because a sight-size

Making relative measurements

If you are not working sight-size, establish a "key" size, such as the width of the mug here, and relate the other objects to it. Make sure to hold the pencil at arm's length each time, as the measurements will not be accurate unless your hand is always exactly the same distance from the objects.

2 *With the first measurements marked in, the artist worked in the normal way, that is, with both eyes open. Only when he saw that something was not quite right in his drawing did he take further measurements, such as the height of the objects and the width of the ellipses.*

drawing can be very small. You can test this out in the same way as before, but this time hold the sketchbook close to the mug first and then about a metre away – the mug will become very small in relation to the paper. Drawing as small as this can be inhibiting – in a life class, for example, the model may be some distance away from you and, if you want to draw boldly in charcoal, sight-size will place unnecessary restrictions on your approach. In such cases you can still use systems of measuring, but you need to establish one "key" size and check everything else against this.

In a figure drawing the head is taken as the unit of measurement – there is more about human proportions later – but in any

drawing some major feature will help you work out relative sizes. In a drawing of an interior, for example, there may be a table or other piece of furniture which plays an important part in the composition. If you draw this in lightly first, you can then work out the scale of other features, such as the height and width of a window behind it, again by holding up a pencil. Try this out with the mug on the table again; first measure the height and then check the relative width. When not drawing sight-size, you must hold the pencil at arm's length and make sure you are always in the same position – the measurements will change as soon as you bend your arm or move forwards or backwards.

DRAWING SHAPES

Drawing involves, among other things, defining a shape by means of its outline, a fact which immediately establishes a kind of falsehood because no object is flat and there are no true outlines in nature. However, we still have to invent this outline because it gives us the shape.

Improve your observational skills by setting up a group of household objects and drawing them first as positive and then as negative shapes.

MAKING AN OUTLINE DRAWING
It is not a bad idea to practise drawing shapes by setting up a simple group of still life objects – perhaps a mug, a plate and a bottle – and approaching them as two-dimensional shapes, drawing them in outline alone. This is not normally the way to make a good drawing because, although it may be accurate in terms of shape, there will be no suggestion of form and the objects will not look solid. However, it is a useful exercise as it does force you to look carefully and to analyse the shapes.

MAKING COMPARISONS
Drawing outlines becomes much easier when you begin to compare one shape against another and to check the relative sizes, as explained on the previous pages. Look, for example, at the way the shapes relate to one another. If you have placed them so that they overlap, how and at what point do they do this? Ask yourself how much larger, taller or wider one shape is than another, and in the case of a tall object such as a bottle, what the proportion of width to height is. A common fault is to treat each part of the drawing in isolation; it is no good drawing a perfectly shaped apple if it is too big for the plate on which it sits.

Drawing outlines

1 *This form of drawing is not easy and you will have to make corrections, so use a medium that allows this. The artist is drawing with a brush and acrylic paint, which she can correct by overpainting in white.*

2 *Drawing an ellipse is difficult at the best of times, but even more so when you can only draw the top half. However, by looking carefully at the subject, the artist has managed well.*

3 *(Right) The drawing of the spoon and ladle was not satisfactory, so white paint is now used to paint out the incorrect lines.*

4 *The white paint does not completely cover the black, and a ghost line remains, which can be a helpful guide when correcting the drawing. If you erase completely, as you would in a pencil drawing, you are likely to repeat exactly the same mistake.*

NEGATIVE SHAPES

Another useful way to check the accuracy of a drawing is to look at the shapes between and behind the objects, known as negative shapes or negative space. If you are drawing a mug with a handle, forget about the handle itself and try to assess the shape of the piece of space between it and the edge of the mug. It can be helpful to draw these shapes before you turn to the positive ones; sometimes you may not have to draw the actual objects at all.

Drawing the negative shapes only is another exercise often set by art teachers and, although it seems slightly perverse, it helps you to sharpen your observational skills. It is also enjoyable, as it forces you to look at things in a completely different way and thus abandon any preconceptions. When your drawings become more ambitious, you can still use these systems of checking and comparing. Negative shapes are very useful in figure drawings, for example, when something has gone wrong but you are not sure what. In a standing pose with arms akimbo, you may have struggled so hard to describe the difficult forms of the limbs that you have failed to relate them properly to the body. You can often discover the mistake by checking the shapes of the spaces between arms and body.

Drawing negative shapes

1 *Again using a brush and acrylic paint, the artist is now drawing the still-life group "in negative", that is, she is painting only the shapes between the objects.*

2 *Drawing in this way involves an initial effort of will, but it can simplify matters. Once you have trained yourself to look for the negative shapes, such as those made by the handles here, they can be easier to recognize than the objects themselves.*

3 *As in the previous drawing, the artist uses white paint to make corrections. It is almost impossible to get every-thing right the first time in this kind of drawing.*

4 *Apart from helping you to observe carefully, drawing negative shapes has another function – it teaches you to consider the relationship of one shape to another, and thus to compose your work. This drawing, although not completely accurate, is lively and full of interest because of the balance between the light and dark shapes.*

DRAWING FORM

So far we have looked at systems of measuring and checking to produce accurate outlines, shapes and proportions, but there is, of course, more to it than this. Drawing is a matter of creating illusions – you are portraying a three-dimensional world in two dimensions, and a good drawing must give a convincing impression of the three-dimensional form of an object as well as its outline.

JUDGING LIGHT AND DARK

Unfortunately no system of measuring can help you to describe the solidity of an object; here you must rely on direct observation, and this is less easy than it sounds. Form is described by the light that falls on an object, which creates light and

For this exercise you need a selection of rounded objects, preferably lit from the side to create well-defined areas of light and dark.

1 *Working entirely with the side of the charcoal stick, and thus avoiding the temptation to use line, the artist begins by blocking in the shapes of the various vegetables.*

2 *Again using a short length of thick willow charcoal held on its side, she builds up the darker area of the aubergine (eggplant).*

3 *The deep shadow between the two vegetables creates a dark line, so here the tip of the charcoal is used. Because charcoal is soft and smudgy, however, it does not give the impression of an outline.*

4 *A finger tip is used to rub off some of the charcoal, creating soft highlights.*

5 *The dimples at the top of the green pepper create rapid transitions of light to dark, so the shadows are deepened with the tip of the charcoal.*

6 *Because charcoal does not adhere well to smooth paper – the artist is working on cartridge (drawing) paper – dark areas often need to be re-established and emphasized towards the end of the drawing.*

7 *Another danger with charcoal drawings is that the highlights can become lost through smudging, but this is easily remedied by the lifting-out technique. It has been used here for the two main highlights on the aubergine (eggplant) and the smaller ones on the top of the pepper.*

dark areas whose shapes depend on the character of the object.

If we lived in a black-and-white world it would be relatively easy to assess these differences in tone (the lightness or darkness of a colour), but more or less anything you choose to draw, whether it be a face or an apple on a plate, has colour. This confuses the issue, because our eyes register colour rather than tone, making it difficult to place the light and dark areas. It helps to half-close your eyes, which blurs the colour and cuts out much of the detail, allowing you to see more clearly in terms of tone.

FORM AND OUTLINE
Outline can be distinctly unhelpful when building up the impression of form, because a hard outline around a shape immediately makes it look flat. The outline of a round or cylindrical object, such as an apple or mug, delineates the boundaries of the form, that is, where it begins to turn away from you; if you put more emphasis on this than on the nearest part of the object, then the illusion of solidity is destroyed.

A good way to practise drawing form is to use tone from the beginning, avoiding outline altogether if you can, or drawing just a light outline for guidance. Try working with a broad medium such as charcoal used sideways, or try the lifting-out method. Of course you don't have to use charcoal – form can be described perfectly well in pencil or even pen and ink – but charcoal will help you to avoid a linear approach.

DRAWING WITH LINE

Having just explained how form is built up with tone, it may seem contradictory now to say that you can create an impression of three dimensions with line alone. It all depends on the quality of the line and how you vary it in your picture – whether it is solid and dark, light and delicate or soft and scarcely visible.

LOST AND FOUND EDGES

As we have seen, drawing a hard outline around something destroys its solidity because objects don't have hard outlines. Some of the edges may be relatively well defined because there is a shadow beneath, but others will be very soft and sometimes difficult to distinguish. These "lost-and-found" edges are an important concept in drawing, as they define volume. You can see the effect even on the simplest object, while more complex ones, such as flowers or the human face, are a mass of hard and soft edges caused by the different characters of the forms and the way they turn away from the light. By accurately observing these differences in line quality, you can produce a drawing which describes form without using any kind of shading. Although not easy to do, it is worth practising, as the results can be very expressive.

Observing edge qualities

A combination of lost-and-found edges can be discerned in any object, depending on the lighting, the shapes and colour. If you can reproduce them accurately, you will be able to draw with line alone.

1 *Using medium willow charcoal, the artist begins with a light drawing, and is now strengthening the found edges on the sugar container.*

2 *She continues to clarify the edges, smudging the charcoal where softer lines are needed, such as in this shadow area. Edges at the bottoms of objects are often almost lost.*

3 (Right) *Although there is no shading on the objects, the drawing gives a convincing impression of three-dimensional form, due partly to the lost-and-found edges and partly to the accurate drawing of the shapes, particularly the ellipses.*

Drawing with contours

1 To make this kind of drawing, it is helpful to restrict yourself to a medium which does not lend itself to shading. The artist is using a fine reed pen and black ink.

2 Having drawn in the basic outline of the model's head and upper body, she begins to add details such as the shirt collar and dangling spectacles.

3 Observing the lines made by the cuffs and the folds at the bent elbows has allowed the artist to describe the arms with no need to use shading.

4 Although not yet finished, the drawing is beginning to give a good impression of shape and form.

5 Pattern is a useful aid in the context of form, and here you can see how the behaviour of the pattern helps to explain the curves of the shoulders and the position of the arms.

6 The majority of drawings are a combination of line and tone, but it can be instructive to restrict yourself to line on occasion. Like all kinds of drawing exercises, this one gives you valuable practice in analysing your subject.

CONTOURS

These are another way of using line to describe form. Contours are not the same as outlines; they are lines that follow the shape of the form. An obvious example would be a pattern curving around a piece of china; less obvious contours are provided by clothing – perhaps the sleeve of a shirt forming a series of folds and creases which define the form below, or the criss-cross of laces on a pair of shoes. Indeed, the clothed human figure provides a wealth of contours, from the line of a waistband indicating the curve of the body, to the cuff of a sleeve or a watch strap explaining the structure of the wrist. Not all objects, of course, provide such convenient clues to form – it would be difficult to describe an apple with contour lines – but, if they are there, try to use them in your picture, whether you draw with line alone or with line and tone together.

SKETCHING

There is no real difference between sketching and drawing, but the word sketch implies a quick study made either for pleasure or for reference, while a drawing can be a finished work with its own pictorial aims. There is, or can be, however, a difference between sketching for its own sake and making studies to be used as reference for another work, whether a finished drawing or a painting.

COLLECTING VISUAL MATERIAL

Artists often go through their sketchbooks to get ideas for compositions or simply to refresh their memories on some detail of a scene. The more you sketch, the more reference material you will have, and sketching also helps to polish up your observational skills. In some cases, however, sketches are made not randomly but to gather material for a composition, in which case it is necessary to consider the kind of visual notes required.

Choosing a sketchbook
(Above) *The kind of sketchbook you require depends on your method of working and the kind of visual notes you wish to make. Some artists have two or three in different sizes and formats. John Townend uses a large book for coloured-pencil drawings like this, and a smaller one for pen-and-ink drawings.*

Sketching for painting
(Left) *This sketch by Stephen Crowther was made as the first stage in planning an oil painting, and the artist has made copious written notes to remind him of the colours. Using a large spiral-bound sketchbook enables him to remove the sheet and pin it up near his easel.*

Choosing the medium

(Far left) *When you are out sketching it is wise to take a selection of different drawing media, as you may find that a particular subject is better suited to one than another. John Townend likes coloured pencil for landscapes, but prefers pen and ink for architectural subjects, where colour is less important than line.*

Collecting ideas

(Left) *David Cuthbert does not make sketches with a specific painting in mind, but he has several sketchbooks in which he notes down anything he sees, often taking photographs at the same time so that he has a store of possible ideas to hand.*

Making colour notes

(Below) *Gerry Baptist works mainly in acrylic, using vivid colours, and his watercolour sketches reflect his artistic preoccupations; a monochrome pencil sketch would therefore not provide the information that he needs for his paintings.*

Depending on the kind of work you are planning, you may need sketches in colour and tone as well as in line. Trying to make a painting from a line sketch in pencil or pen and ink is virtually impossible; you will have no idea what colour the sky was or which areas were dark and which ones light. It is wise to make a habit of including all the information possible on your sketches – if you don't have time to sketch in colour, make written notes about the colours. Do not simply write "blue" or "green", but try to analyse the colours; as long as you can understand the notes, this can be more valuable than sketching in colour, particularly if you intend to use one medium for the sketches and another for the painting. A sketch in coloured pencil, for example, would be very difficult to translate into watercolour or oil.

MATERIALS

For sketching you can use any drawing media with which you feel comfortable. Pencil is a good all-rounder, as it allows you to establish tone as well as line. Pen and ink

is useful for small sketches, but less so for tonal studies. Coloured pencils are tailor-made for colour sketches, and so are pastels and oil pastels, although neither of the latter is suitable for small-scale work. You can buy large sketching pads containing different colours of pastel paper, or you can clip pieces of paper to a drawing board.

Sketchbooks, usually containing cartridge (drawing) paper, can be bought in many shapes and sizes. Unless you like to work small, don't be tempted by a tiny address-book size, as you may find that it restricts and frustrates you.

FIGURE DRAWING

The old saying that "If you can paint people you can paint anything" reflects the fact that the human figure is one of the most challenging of all subjects, whether you are drawing or painting. The importance of figure study as a training ground for aspiring artists was recognized in the past, when drawing from life formed an important part of any art student's education. Nowadays there is less emphasis on it, at any rate in art schools, but amateurs flock to life classes, and many professionals return to them at stages during their careers to brush up their skills.

Joining a life class is not essential if you intend to restrict yourself to the clothed figure or to portrait studies; you can usually find someone who is willing to pose for you, or you can draw yourself in a mirror. However, for nude studies you must have a model as well as a decent-sized room in which to draw, so a class is the best answer; alternatively, you could share the cost of a model with friends or colleagues.

THE PROPORTIONS OF THE FIGURE

In the main, drawing is learned by practice, not from books, but books can provide some advice and point out things you may overlook when drawing. Figure drawings often go wrong because the proportions are not properly understood and, although human figures vary greatly, it is helpful to bear in mind some basic rules. These will prevent you from making heads and feet too small – a common error – and help you to analyse what is special about the body you are drawing.

Allowing for individual differences, the human body is approximately seven-and-a-half heads high. The mid-point of the body is slightly above the genital area, with one

Proportions
Although the general rule is that the body is about seven-and-a-half heads high, it is essential to remember that there are variations; this model's head is relatively large. Observing these individual differences will give authenticity to your drawings.

Checking angles
In a pose like this it is important to represent accurately the slope of the shoulders and hips. Establish the precise angle by holding your pencil at arm's length and adjusting it until it coincides, then take it carefully down to the paper and mark in the line.

Checking balance
The centre of balance is vital in a standing pose, and you can check this either with a pencil or a plumbline, as shown here. This is a slightly laborious method, but is more accurate than holding up a pencil, where there is a danger of tilting it away from the vertical.

quarter point above the nipples and the other just below the knees. If arms are hanging loose by the side of the body, the wrists will be below the mid-point of the body, with the fingertips reaching to mid-thigh. The hand is about the same length as the face, from chin to forehead – try this out by covering your own face with your hand – and the length of the foot is approximately equal to the whole height of the head.

FORESHORTENING

In figure drawing, the head is always used as the unit of measurement, enabling you to make comparative measurements. Measuring systems become particularly important when the figure, or any parts of it, are foreshortened. Foreshortening is the perspective effect which causes things to appear larger the nearer they are; in a reclining figure, seen from the feet end, the feet will be large and the legs very short. It can be difficult to assess the effects of foreshortening accurately, partly because you know a leg is a certain length and find it hard to believe what you see, and partly because the forms themselves often change. In a seated figure seen from the front the thighs will be wide and short, because the flesh is pushed out by the body's weight.

Some degree of foreshortening is generally present in figure drawing and, because the effects created are often surprising, it is vital to take measurements. As you draw, hold your pencil out at arm's length to check the relative lengths and widths of limbs and body, returning to the head as the basic unit of measurement.

BALANCE AND WEIGHT

You can also use the outstretched pencil method to check angles, another common problem area. The angle of the shoulders or

(Left) *The balance line will fall nearer one foot than the other according to the way in which the weight is distributed.*

(Right) *Here the weight is mainly on one foot, with a little of it taken by the hand resting on the table.*

Drawing movement

(Right) *To depict the figure in motion, a difficult but rewarding subject, you need a medium which actively discourages detail. In Arms Swing Hil Scott has drawn with a brush and diluted Chinese ink, adding touches of charcoal line. The definition is minimal, yet the drawing is an elegant description of the fluid lines of body and arms.*

(Left) *Here the weight is divided between the arm and the right leg, and the shoulders and hips slope in opposite directions.*

(Below) *Very little weight is taken by the feet in this stance, so the balance line falls some way outside them.*

tilt of the hips often provides the key to the pose. In a standing figure with the weight on one leg, for example, the shoulders and hips slope in opposite directions; whenever one part of the body moves, another does so in compensation, to maintain the balance. Hold out your pencil and align it with the shoulder or hip line and then, very carefully, take the pencil down to the drawing and mark in the angle as a guide line.

In a standing pose, "balance lines" can be helpful; these give you the position of the feet in relation to the body. It is vital that this is correct, as your drawing will not look convincing unless you convey an impression of the way in which the body's weight is distributed, and the feet, of course, are the bearers of the weight.

Choosing the right medium

(Right) *Children are notoriously restless and usually have to be drawn very fast. It is thus wise to choose a medium which enables you to work quickly and broadly. Ted Gould has used brown Conté crayon for his lovely* Mother and Child, *suggesting both form and detail with a few deft touches.*

Balance lines are taken from the middle of the neck in a front or back view, and from the ear in a side view, down to the feet. If the model is standing with the weight evenly distributed, the balance line will be between the feet, but if most of the weight is on one leg it will be considerably nearer the weight-bearing foot. The most accurate way to provide yourself with these vertical references is to use a plumbline, which simply consists of a piece of string with a weight at one end.

The way in which the distribution of weight affects the body is less obvious in a seated pose, but it is equally important to identify it, or the drawing will look stiff and unnatural. Here again it is essential to check alignments, either with a pencil or a plumbline. You can either use the same system of balance lines or mark in a central

The standing figure

(Right) *As explained on the previous pages it is vital to analyse the pose and to understand how the weight is distributed and how the whole body is affected by any movement. In his two brush-and-wash drawings James Horton captures beautifully both the swing of the body, and also its three-dimensional quality of mass and weight.*

Composing the drawing
(Left) *Drawings can be made for practice, or they can simply be sketches of something which happens to take your fancy. A drawing, however, can also be carried out with the intention of producing a finished work, in which case you must consider composition. Paul Bartlett's* Father with Lamp *is as carefully composed as any painting, with the sweeping curves of the figure, chair and writing pad balanced by the table and the dark upright of the lamp.*

vertical line to which you can relate the position of the feet, head and various parts of the torso.

THE CLOTHED FIGURE

Drawing people with their clothes on is perhaps slightly easier than drawing the nude, if only because there is more opportunity to practise. You don't need a "proper" model because you can draw people anywhere as long as you restrict yourself to quick sketches. For more thorough and detailed studies, friends and family may oblige, indeed many people are flattered to be asked to pose.

Clothing can be helpful in defining the forms beneath it, providing a set of contour lines, but it can also disguise form and confuse the issue in a bewildering way. A thin garment, for example, reveals the body, while a heavy overcoat gives little idea as to the shapes beneath or to the way its wearer is sitting or standing. In such cases you must look for clues, such as the angle of a protruding wrist and hand, the bend of an elbow or the slope of the shoulders.

Whatever kind of garments your subject is wearing, try to visualize the body beneath. Analyse the pose just as you would in a nude study, taking measurements and checking alignments of head, shoulders, feet and so on, and perhaps drawing in some light guidelines to indicate key points, even if you can't see them. Clothing can be difficult to draw; it often forms complicated shapes of its own and you can become so involved with drawing folds, or the pattern on a fabric, that you fail to make sense of the figure itself.

Rounded forms

(Above) *This simple pencil drawing by Elisabeth Harden concentrates on the rounded nature of the female form. The relaxed pose of the model and raised left leg are depicted in a flowing outline, with no sharp angles used at all.*

Composing with shapes

(Opposite) *In his pastel drawing,* Elly, *David Cuthbert has made an exciting composition by reducing detail and concentrating on the interplay of shapes – the curves of the limbs counterpointing the more geometric shapes of the clothing and chair.*

Drawing light

(Right) *Forms are described by the way in which the light falls on them, so in life drawing or portraiture it helps to have a fairly strong source of illumination. In Gerry Baptist's simple but powerful charcoal drawing, the light comes from one side, slightly behind the model, making a lovely pale shape across the shoulders and down the hip and leg.*

Focus on Figure

PASTEL DEMONSTRATION

D
R
A
W
I
N
G

James Horton is primarily a landscape painter, working mainly in oils, but for drawings he frequently uses pastels, which he finds particularly well suited to figure work. Pastel is both a drawing and a painting medium, depending on how it is used, and he exploits its linear qualities, building up colours with light layers of hatching and crosshatching so that each line remains distinct. He avoids the techniques closely associated with pastel painting, such as side strokes, blending and overlaying layers of thick, solid colour.

1 *Because pastels cannot easily be erased it is important to begin with an accurate drawing. This is made with a stick of compressed charcoal; pencil should not be used for pastel work, as the slight greasiness of the graphite repels the pastel colour.*

2 *The artist begins by placing small areas of colour all over the picture, relating the rich background colours to the subtler flesh tints. The coloured paper (Ingres) provides a middle tone, making it easier to work up to the highlights and down to the darks.*

3 *This stage clearly illustrates his method of hatching and cross-hatching. He holds the pastel stick lightly and takes care to vary the lines so that they do not all go in the same direction.*

4 (Right) *The colours are gradually built up, but the first colours are allowed to show through each application, creating a network of lines and marks which gives a livelier effect than smooth blends.*

5 *At this stage much of the paper is still uncovered, but it does not need to be covered completely, as the light greenish-brown is very close to the colour of the shadows on the flesh. Choosing the right paper colour is an important aspect of pastel work.*

6 *The compressed charcoal is used again to darken and define areas of the hair and to sharpen up the drawing. Charcoal mixes well with pastel, and can be a better choice than black pastel, which makes solid and sometimes over-assertive black lines.*

7 (Above) *The process of building up the darker colours and defining details continues, with brown pastel now used lightly to draw the side of the arm. On the shoulder, some of the original charcoal drawing is still visible, and has been strengthened by curving lines of red-brown pastel behind it.*

8 (Below) *The artist has not attempted to treat the background or foreground in detail, concentrating instead on the rich, golden colours of the body. This vignetting method, in which the focal point of the picture is emphasized by allowing the surrounding colours to merge gently into the toned paper, is a traditional pastel-drawing technique.*

ANIMALS

D
R
A
W
I
N
G

Drawing animals can be rewarding and
frustrating in equal measure. Whether
they are wild creatures, farm animals or
household pets, animals make wonderful
subjects – it is enjoyable simply watching
them – but unfortunately they are not the
most co-operative of models. Even cats,
which generally sleep for long periods, have
a tendency to wake up and walk away as
soon as you reach for your sketchbook.
However, many artists have portrayed
animals successfully, purely because
they were fascinated by them, and this
should be your sole criterion in choosing
your subject matter.

OBSERVATION AND SKETCHING

As with any branch of drawing, the secret
lies in careful observation of detail, the
determination not to be put off by failures
and, most important of all in this context,
the ability to tailor your methods to your
subject. You will certainly not be able to
produce the kind of finished drawing you
might achieve with a figure or an
architectural subject, but you can make
quick sketches, and a good sketch often says
more than any amount of detail and polish.

You may find it difficult at first, because
it does require some practice to be able to
grasp the essentials of a subject and get
them down on paper in a few minutes, or
maybe just a few seconds. However, you
will find that even your first, perhaps not
very successful sketches will have sharpened
your observational skills, and the next
sketches will be better for this reason.
Sketching is a knack, and it really does
become easier the more you do it. Use a
medium you know you can control well and
one that enables you to work quickly in
both line and tone – soft pencil, Conté
crayon or pastel are all suitable.

**Rhythm and
movement**
(Above) *In an animal
drawing, as in a figure
study, it is important to
convey the living quality
of the creature and the
way it moves, so choose
a medium which allows
you to work rapidly and
freely. Judy Martin's* Cat
Study *is a large-scale
drawing: she likes to
work "from the elbow",
and has drawn directly
with a brush and acrylic
paint. The diagonal
placing of the animal on
the paper, together with
the sweeping curve of
the tail, give a strong
sense of movement.*

Drawing texture
*Texture, whether the rough, shaggy hair of a dog, the
soft fur of a cat or the lustrous plumage of a bird, is
one of the most attractive features of animal subjects,
but you cannot concentrate on these qualities when
you are trying to draw animals in motion so you will
often have to work from photographs or museum
specimens. In his pencil drawing* Dead Bird *Robert
Maxwell Wood has taken advantage of the mortality
of all creatures, to provide himself with an excellent
subject for close study.*

Shape and pattern

(Right) *This pencil drawing is a preliminary design for a print, a medium in which three-dimensional form is less important than the arrangement of shapes. What first attracted Elisabeth Harden to the subject was the shapes of the animals' markings, which she has stressed with firm outlines and shading.*

Multiple drawings

(Far right) *Animals tend to repeat their movements, and another approach is to do several drawings on one page and work on them at the same time, as Vicky Lowe has done in her brush-and-wash studies of rabbits. Not only does this help in practical terms, as you can move on to another drawing as soon as the creature moves, but it also creates an impression similar to an animated cartoon.*

REPEATED MOVEMENTS

There is an element of memory involved in drawing anything in motion, particularly if the movement is rapid, because our eyes simply can't keep up with it. There is no one split second in which you can say "Ah, that's what the legs are doing." It is interesting to note that even the great 18th-century British artist George Stubbs, who specialized in horses, was unable to portray them convincingly in motion. It was not until the era of photography that the sequence of movements made by a galloping horse was fully understood. Now that we know how a horse moves, it is much easier to appreciate the repetitive nature of most animals' movements. Look for these repeated movements when you are sketching, making several small sketches on the same page so that you have a complete visual record of all the different positions of the legs and body.

PHOTOGRAPHIC REFERENCE

The advent of photographs was invaluable to the 19th-century painters in correcting misconceptions about movement, and they still play an important part in providing reference for drawings and paintings. If you want to draw wild animals – which seldom even appear to order, let alone stay still – photographs are generally the only option available for reference.

Keeping up with movement

(Left) *Even when quietly grazing, animals will shift their weight from one leg to another and make other small changes in their position. Do not try to change your drawing each time; instead simply draw one line over another, as Karen Raney has done in her coloured-ink drawing of* French Horses. *As can be seen, she has begun with light lines and washes, and has delayed finalizing the positions of limbs and feet with more positive colours until the later stages.*

COLOURED-PENCIL DEMONSTRATION

Judy Martin is not a professional animal artist; indeed she sees herself primarily as an abstract painter. She has, however, always been fascinated by animals, and at one point in her career drew and painted little else. From time to time she returns to such subjects with enjoyment, working mainly from photographs but always inter-preting photographic reference in order to create her own compositions and colours. Here a photograph is used as the basis for the cat, but the background and foreground are imaginary.

1 *Here the artist is working with water-soluble pencils on watercolour paper. She begins by laying some light lines and then washes over them. This releases some of the colour and softens the pencil marks without disturbing them.*

2 *A different effect is created by dipping the pencil into water before applying it. As you can see, this produces a more solid area of colour.*

3 *With dry coloured pencils, dark colours have to be deepened gradually, but water-soluble pencils make it easier to establish the dark tones at an early stage.*

4 *With the dark and light tones of the cat established, the artist can now consider the background. A solid area of colour on the left is needed to provide a balance for the animal, plus a contrast of textures, so here she uses the pencil dry.*

5 *Warm reddish browns have been introduced with a dry pencil to suggest the texture of the fur. A wet grey pencil creates a soft effect on the tail.*

7 (Right) *Building up a complex pattern is a slow process and it is easy to make mistakes; to guard against this, a tracing is made from the completed area and the lines transferred to the working surface.*

6 (Above) *The dark background has been completed, with black cross-hatched over the blue, and a patterned cloth (which was not in the photograph) has been invented to create some interest in the foreground. As it is difficult to work without visual reference, a piece of fabric from the artist's collection of still-life draperies provided the basis for the pattern.*

8 *With the background and patterned cloth finished, the artist returns to the focal point of the picture, and builds up detail and texture with a combination of wet-and-dry applications of pencil.*

9 *Finally, she uses white gouache paint and a small brush to touch in the whiskers. Coloured pencils are less opaque than either pastels or gouache paints, so clear whites cannot be produced by drawing over dark colours with white pencil.*

10 *In any finished drawing, the composition is as important as the representation of the subject; here careful planning has balanced the elongated shape of the cat's body with the patterned cloth and the dark rectangle of the background.*

BUILDINGS

The man-made environment of cities, towns and villages provides a wealth of varied and exciting drawing subjects, whether you are interested in architectural styles or simply in atmosphere. It is sometimes thought that drawing buildings is a special skill, but, although detailed "architectural renderings" are specialized and have a particular purpose, buildings and townscapes present no more of a problem than any other subject, and are almost certainly easier than drawing the nude figure. What puts many people off is the word "perspective" – most of us know that linear perspective is based on mathematics and, for those of us who failed to grasp geometry at school, that is quite enough to cause alarm and despondency.

CONVERGING PARALLELS

It is true that the laws of perspective were arrived at originally through mathematics, but it is not true that they cannot be understood by non-mathematical people. The basic rules are really very simple, and they always bear out the evidence of your own eyes. Most people must at some time have walked or driven down a straight road and noticed how the two sides converge in the distance. This apparent meeting of receding parallel lines is one of the many tricks the eye plays with reality – the lines don't really meet, but in visual terms they do, and drawing is concerned with what we see. Without perspective it would be impossible to create the illusion of our three-dimensional surroundings on a flat piece of paper.

As parallel lines appear to come closer and closer together until they meet, it follows that things get smaller the further away they are. Imagine a row of identical buildings along the road. If you were to

draw one line through the top of the roofs and another below the doors, they would be receding parallel lines too, and would meet at the same place as those for the sides of the road, with the houses becoming smaller and smaller. Again, the effect of this law of diminishing size is something that everyone must have observed.

VANISHING POINTS

The place where the parallel lines meet is called the vanishing point, for obvious reasons, and it is located on an imaginary line called the horizon. This is the most important fact of all because, although the line is imaginary, it isn't arbitrary – it is your own eye level. This is why perspective changes as soon as you move your own

Central vanishing point
(Above) *The drawing has been done from a central position, so the vanishing point is also in the centre, with the receding parallel lines sloping down to the horizon line, which is at the level of the artist's eye. In fact the receding lines at the top of the drawing are not entirely correct – they should slope more steeply – but drawings can often be the better for small inaccuracies in the perspective.*

Moving position

(Right) *The artist has now moved to the left in order to see more of the right-hand wall, and the vanishing point has also changed position. The horizon, however, remains constant, as this drawing has been done from the same level as the first one.*

viewpoint, even from a sitting to a standing position. You have changed the horizon, the vanishing point and the direction of the parallel lines.

There is, of course, one further complication: there are often two or more different vanishing points, depending on your angle of viewing. If you are drawing a house from an angle, both planes will be receding from you, so lines drawn through the tops and bottoms of each would meet at their own separate vanishing points. In an old town or village, houses may be set at odd angles to each other, resulting in many different vanishing points.

PERSPECTIVE BY EYE

In such cases you cannot possibly establish the exact position of each vanishing point, but it is important to mark in the horizon line and, if possible, the vanishing point for one key building of the scene before you. You can work out the other receding lines by holding up a pencil or ruler and tilting it

Two vanishing points

(Left) *The majority of architectural subjects have at least two different vanishing points, depending on how many planes there are and the angle from which they are viewed. Here there are two, with the converging parallels sloping more sharply down to the horizon line on the right. All three drawings, by John Townend, are in pen and ink.*

Continued ▷

Perspective and proportion

(Left) *In Paul Bartlett's pen-and-ink drawing, a study made for a painting, the perspective is impressively accurate, as is the observation of the building's proportions. Notice the care taken over the number of bars in each window and the exact size of each brick and roof tile.*

Shapes and colours

(Below) *Town scenes, which present a variety of different elements, provide an opportunity to explore contrasts of shape, surface texture and colour. In his sketchbook study in coloured pencil, David Cuthbert's interest has been primarily in the lively patterns made by the buildings, street furniture, flags and shadows.*

Interiors

(Below) *The inside of a building is as interesting and rewarding to draw as the exterior, and you have the additional bonus of being protected both from the weather and inquisitive eyes. In his pen-and-ink drawing* The Church Organ Before Renovation *John Townend has made an exciting composition based mainly on the interplay of curves and diagonal lines.*

until it coincides with the angles of the roof, window tops or other features, as explained under figure drawing.

You do not have to get all the vanishing points exactly right – indeed this will be impossible, as many of them may be outside the picture area – but do make checks from time to time if you see something that doesn't look right. If you misjudge one angle and try to relate all the others to it the drawing will become distorted. And if you are bad at drawing straight lines don't be afraid to use a ruler, at least at the start of a drawing. Vertical lines really do have to be vertical in architectural subjects.

SCALE AND PROPORTION

Proportion is every bit as important as perspective – perhaps even more so. While it is correct (or reasonably correct) perspective which makes a drawing look realistic and the building not about to fall over, it is well-observed proportion which conveys character. You would not expect to draw a portrait without paying attention to the size of your sitter's eyes in relation to his

Buildings as a setting
(Left) *In Gerald Cains's mixed-media drawing* Open End, Ashton Gate *(in acrylic, watercolour and ink) it is the people who claim attention rather than buildings, which merely provide an urban setting. He has created a very powerful and rather sinister effect by playing with scale; the foreground figures on the steps dwarf their surroundings.*

Composition
(Below) *Making a finished drawing from sketches or photographs gives you more chance to adjust reality. Ray Evans sketches continually to amass a store of visual information, and when he makes finished drawings he often combines elements from several sketchbook studies. His* Port Isaac *is in pen and watercolour.*

or her face, but it is surprising how many people ignore the importance of the size of windows and doors, or the heights of roofs in relation to walls.

When drawing a designed building such as a historic cathedral or fine country house, such factors are naturally taken into account, because the grand scale of the building or the carefully planned balance of the architectural features are the principal attractions of the subject. But scale and proportion are always important, even when your subject is an old wooden barn or a higgledy-piggledy collection of cottages or town houses; these are the characteristics which will give your drawing a convincing "sense of place".

Relative sizes can be measured by holding up a pencil at arm's length and moving your thumb up and down it, but if you are drawing sight-size you can be more accurate by using a ruler to read off the actual measurements. Work out the height of the building in relation to its width, the proportion of wall to roof, and the number and size of the windows. Don't forget that the laws of diminishing size make the spaces between windows become smaller as they recede, as well as the windows themselves – this is a trap for the unwary. Be particularly

careful with doors, as they will look structurally impossible if they are too small, and bizarre if they are too large – doors are designed so that the average person can pass comfortably in and out without having to stoop or walk in sideways. People in a townscape give an indication of scale as well as creating a feeling of atmosphere, but make sure that the doors you put in can accommodate them.

MIXED-MEDIA DEMONSTRATION

D
R
A
W
I
N
G

Karen Raney is an artist who enjoys experimenting with different media and different techniques, in both her drawings and her paintings. Her subject matter is as varied as her methods, but as a city dweller she is particularly interested in the challenge and stimulation of urban scenes. She uses photographs as a starting point when it is not possible to work direct from the subject – which can be difficult in towns and cities – but does so selectively, rejecting any elements in the photograph which she does not require for her composition.

1 *The artist intends to use a version of the sgraffito technique in combination with pencil and Conté crayon. She has begun by scribbling all over the paper with an oil bar, which is similar to a thick, soft oil pastel. Having drawn over this with Conté crayon, she now applies more in selected areas.*

2 *The Conté crayon is smudged with a finger so that it mixes into the layers of oil bar beneath. The oil and the texture of the heavy watercolour paper have broken up the Conté marks, creating a nice soft effect.*

3 *Conté crayon is now inscribed more heavily over the first applications of oil and crayon. The drawing is kept loose and free at this stage, with the shapes evolving very gradually.*

4 *The Conté has been applied quite heavily over the oil crayon, and the corner of a plastic card is employed, firstly to scratch into it and then to re-apply the resulting mixture of oil and Conté, which has become rather like paint.*

5 *The composition is allowed to emerge gradually,
as the artist wished to establish the foreground
before deciding on how many of the background
buildings to include. She now uses a soft pencil to
mark the side of a more distant building.*

6 *(Right) Detailed definition will be left until
the final stages; concentration now is on the
composition, the main perspective lines and the
distribution of lights and darks.*

7 *Some of the lines are strengthened with soft
pencil. In this photograph you can clearly see the
effect of scratching and scraping with the plastic card,
particularly in the foreground.*

8 *A further
application of
oil bar again mixes
with the Conté crayon
beneath to produce a
soft paste which can
be manipulated
and moved around.*

Continued ▷

9 *The card is used to draw into the paste-like substance. The effect resembles brushmarks in a painting, with the corner of the card making a positive dark line.*

10 (Right) *The picture is sufficiently advanced for the artist to begin work on the details of the buildings, and here she uses a 2B pencil, applying pressure to bite through the thin layer of oil bar.*

11 *To suggest the texture of the building on the left, she has applied a further layer of oil bar and now draws into it, using the pencil lightly so that it only partially dislodges the oily underlayer.*

12 (Above) *A further hint of texture is given by painting over the lines of oil and Conté with white gouache. This also lightens an area which was previously rather too dark.*

13 *With all the details of the foreground buildings now completed, the artist turns her attention to the details in the background. Here she needs a soft effect to suggest distance, so she smudges the Conté-and-oil mixture with her fingertip.*

14 (Opposite) *The finished picture is not only an exciting evocation of a cityscape, it is also fascinating in terms of technique. The repeated layering and scraping of the Conté crayon and oil have produced a wonderful surface texture and density of tone which give the drawing something of the richness of an etching.*

Pastel Painting

Introduction
ABOUT PASTELS

Pastel is unique in that it is both a drawing and a painting medium. It tends to be associated with drawing because the colours are not applied with a brush, but the medium's malleability and richness of colour invite a painterly approach. Many of today's artists exploit this effect in pastel to produce works which at first sight look almost like oil paintings.

Pastel is rapidly becoming one of the most favoured painting media, vying with watercolour for popularity. One of the reasons for this is probably that pastel sticks simply look so beautiful – open one of the boxed sets of pastels in an art shop and you will see a rich array of colours, which seem to offer a direct invitation to the artist. A tube of paint is a poor thing by comparison because you can't see the colour until you have squeezed it out.

JAMES CRITTENDEN
SUMMER HILLSIDE
(Left) *Pastel is often associated with delicate colours, hence the term "pastel shades", but this powerful landscape shows that considerable depth of tone can be achieved by laying one colour over another. The artist has given a lovely feeling of life and energy by the way he has used the pastel strokes; in the trees, particularly, the effect is very much like brushstrokes in an oil or acrylic painting.*

PATRICK CULLEN

WINDOW IN PROVENCE

(Opposite) *The colours are also built up thickly in this painting, but the technique is very different, with short pieces of pastel used to make broader marks. To create the gentle but luminous colours, the artist has restricted himself to light and mid-tones, controlling them carefully, and changing the direction of the strokes to give variety to the different surfaces.*

KEN PAINE

HEAD OF A YOUNG WOMAN

(Right) *This artist exploits the directness and expressive qualities of pastel in his portraits. He works with great rapidity, usually beginning by building up the tonal structure with a monochrome "underpainting" made with broad strokes of short lengths of pastel. Linear definition and bright colour accents are left until the final stages. The coloured paper is still visible in areas.*

MAUREEN JORDAN

ROSE AND GERANIUM TEXTURES

(Below) *The artist has exploited the whole range of pastel techniques in this vivid and lively picture, combining solid, thickly applied colour, blended in places, with fine-line drawing to pick out individual flowers and petals. In the foreground, an area which can become dull in a floral group, a series of strong, decisive marks creates its own pattern and interest.*

PROS AND CONS

The immediacy of pastel is also appealing. These sticks of colour form a direct link between your hand and the paper. You don't have to mix colours on a palette and you need no brushes. Like any drawing medium, pastels are responsive, easy to manipulate and quick to use, which makes them ideal for outdoor work and rapid effects; but because of their loose, crumbly texture and brilliance of colour – pastels are almost pure pigment – they can also be built up thickly in layers just as paints can. As you will see from the small gallery of paintings shown here, pastels are a versatile medium and there are many different ways of using them.

No medium is perfect, however, and those who are not accustomed to pastels may experience some problems until they become familiar with techniques involved, and learn what pastels can and cannot do.

GEOFF MARSTERS
LANDSCAPE IN THE AUVERGNE
(Left) When he first took up pastels, Marsters was determined to use the medium as a painting rather than a drawing technique, and through constant experiment he has evolved his own methods of working. He achieves his rich, dense colours by working on abrasive (pumice) paper, rubbing the pastel into it, fixing and then applying further layers on top. He loves the brilliance of pastels, and exploits this quality by "keying up" the colours.

One of the advantages of pastels – that you do not have to pre-mix colours – can also work against you. Any mixing has to be done on the working surface but, because it is not possible to try out mixes in advance as you can with paints, it is all too easy to make mistakes. You cannot erase pastels easily, although you can correct mistakes to some extent by laying more colours on top. If you do too much of this, however, you will clog the paper surface and may end up with a tired-looking, muddy painting.

One of the greatest exponents of pastel, the 18th-century portrait painter Maurice Quentin de La Tour, mentioned the possibility of spoiling work by over-mixing; he had one or two other complaints, too – about the dust generated by working with pastels, for example. It has to be admitted that it is not a medium for those who like to keep their floors clean. It is hard on the hands too, as they become covered with colour as soon as you pick up a stick.

A more serious problem is the fragility of pastels, in particular soft pastels. The sticks break very easily under pressure, added to which it is very easy to smudge finished work. Even when sprayed with fixative, the pigments tend to fall off the paper,

especially if they rub up against another surface. Unless you can frame and glaze your work immediately, it is vital to store it carefully, laying it flat with pieces of tissue paper on top.

Despite these minor problems, pastel is a wonderful medium to use. Few who have taken it up, whether amateur or professional, feel inclined to abandon it.

PATRICK CULLEN
CASA DE LIDO
(Left) *In this atmospheric painting, the approach to colour is more naturalistic than in the landscape opposite, but there are some similarities in technique, with the pastel again applied thickly and layered in places. Cullen usually works either on sandpaper, or on heavy watercolour paper on which he first lays a ground of watercolour.*

GEOFF MARSTERS
INTERIOR OF BOATHOUSE
(Right) *This subject, with its angularity and profusion of detail, might not seem suitable for a soft, crumbly medium such as pastel, which is usually considered better for broad effects, but the artist has treated it with great assurance. If you look closely you can see that the lines and edges are in fact quite loose and free; the impression of sharp linearity is created by the strong contrasts of tone and colour.*

JACKIE SIMMONDS
STILL LIFE WITH BLUE SPANISH GLASS
(Left) *In this gentle and tranquil painting the artist has made clever use of pastel's capacity for creating a variety of textures. For the glass, deep blues have been blended to imitate the smoothness of the material, but the central area of the plate has been left slightly rough, while in the background several colours have been dragged lightly over one another.*

JACKIE SIMMONDS
TEA ON THE PATIO

(Above) *This delightful painting probably comes closest to most people's idea of pastel – the colours are light and fresh, in keeping with the airy subject, and the handling is delicate. In fact, however, these qualities owe more to the artist's skill in controlling the medium than to its inherent properties; it needs a light touch and a sound knowledge of both colour and technique to achieve such effects.*

ELIZABETH MOORE
STILL LIFE WITH PEARS AND PLUMS

(Below) *For this still life, the artist has worked in oil pastel, which she likes because it is related to oil paint, the medium she uses most frequently. She also finds it more controllable than soft pastel. Here it has allowed her to build up deep, rich colours as well as very subtle effects, notably the bloom on the plums.*

MAUREEN JORDAN
PANSY TEXTURES

(Above) *The characteristic crumbly texture of pastel can benefit from contrast with a smoother medium, and here the artist has used pastel in combination with acrylic. The acrylic underpainting has also allowed her to establish deep, rich colours from the outset without a heavy build-up of pastel.*

JAMES CRITTENDEN
ORANGE GROVE IN THE EVENING

(Left) *As in most of his pastel paintings, this artist skilfully combines the drawing and painting qualities of pastel to produce an interpretation of the landscape that is both realistic and highly personal. What appear at first glance to be solid areas of colour – the sky and grass – are in fact a complex network of overlaid lines and marks made with the tip of the stick, while the leaves of the trees are expressed by rapid calligraphic dashes and squiggles.*

PIP CARPENTER
THE SUN-DAPPLED TABLE

(Right) *This painting, worked on a dark, greenish paper, gives the initial impression of oil pastel, but in fact is soft pastel pressed hard into the paper and fixed between stages to allow one colour to be laid over another. The artist was particularly excited by the effect of the light on the different surfaces – the volume of the fruit and the flat plane of the ornamental iron table.*

JUDY MARTIN
BANDSTAND SERIES

(Left) *Vivid colour was of primary importance in this painting, and here, too, acrylic has been used in combination with pastel. The underpainting, which set the colour-key for the picture, was mainly in shades of red and yellow, with contrasting colours of pastel applied on top in vigorous strokes. You can see this effect clearly in the sky, where strokes of blue pastel overlay bright red paint.*

There are four main types of pastel: soft (also known as chalk pastels), hard pastels, pastel pencils and oil pastels. All pastels are made in the same way. Ground pigment is bulked out with a "filler" such as chalk and held together with some sort of binder, the traditional one being gum tragacanth.

SOFT PASTELS

Very little binder is used in the manufacture of soft pastels, which are almost pure pigment, hence their brilliance of colour, fragility and powdery texture. Although the majority of pastel painters use soft pastels, you may find hard pastels and pastel pencils form a useful complement to these.

HARD PASTELS

Hard pastels contain more binder and have a finer consistency. They do not break so easily and can be sharpened to a fine point for detailed work. Some artists use the side of a hard pastel stick to block in large areas of colour in the preliminary stages of a painting. Because they are less crumbly than soft pastels, they are easier to work over with other colours as the work progresses. They can also be used on their own, but in general they are better suited to pastel drawing, where the approach is more linear, than to pastel painting. The range of colours is also quite limited, at least in comparison with soft pastels, where the colour variations are truly awesome.

PASTEL PENCILS

These are also more of a drawing than a painting tool, but a few pastel pencils will form a useful addition to your kit; they are ideal for small areas of detail in a painting as well as for making preliminary drawings. Ordinary graphite pencils should never be used for underdrawings for pastel, as

graphite is slightly greasy and will repel any pastel colour laid on top. In terms of softness and hardness, pastel pencils lie somewhere in the middle. The colour ranges are similar to those of hard pastels.

OIL PASTELS

These can't be used in combination with ordinary pastels, as they are bound with oil rather than gum. They are, however, an excellent alternative to soft pastels and are capable of very exciting and painterly effects. What is particularly intriguing about them is that the colour can be "melted" with turpentine or white spirit, then spread across the paper with a brush. You can even dip a brush moistened with turpentine into the sticks of colour and apply it, just as you would put on paint. The colours are rather more restricted than those of soft pastels but, as the medium grows in popularity, manufacturers are beginning to respond to demand.

DIFFERENT SHADES

In oil, watercolour and acrylic painting, you can manage with very few basic colours because you can obtain so many more by means of mixing. Pastels, however, can't be premixed, so you will need many more sticks of pastel than you would tubes of paint. Choosing a range of colours which gives you sufficient scope for colour matching, without incurring vast expense, can be a problematical business. Some ranges contain literally hundreds of colours, so where do you start?

Fortunately many manufacturers help you here, producing "starter" sets tailored to particular subject areas. There are, for example, large and small boxed sets, with a range of suitable colours for either landscape or portrait work. One of these

OIL PASTELS

PASTEL PENCILS

SOFT PASTELS

CRUMBLED SOFT PASTELS

could make a good starting point. You can add more colours when you know which ones you need – all pastels are sold singly as well as in boxes.

If you already know something about colour, you can simply rely on choosing by eye. As you look through drawers of pastels, you will notice that some of the colours bear a name and a number. The latter denotes the tone of the colour,

whether it is a light or dark version of ultramarine, for example. All pastel colours are made in a pure hue plus light and dark versions, the former achieved by adding white and the latter by adding black. Unfortunately, there is no standard naming or numbering system among manufacturers but, as you become more experienced, you wil! be able to pick out the colours you want quite quickly.

VARIATIONS

There are considerable differences in colour from one range of pastels to another so, when you have reached the stage of adding colours, it's always worth trying out several different kinds. Experienced artists become familiar with the different ranges and often have one or two favourite colours made only by one particular manufacturer. They will thus have a selection of different makes in their "paintbox".

The textures vary too. Some "soft" pastels are relatively hard, while others are so crumbly that they break as soon as you pick them up and have to be spread with your fingers. You can find these things out only by experience, but it's all part of the learning process.

HARD PASTELS

PASTEL PENCILS

PAPERS

The choice of paper is extremely important in pastel work because both the colour and the texture play an important part in the overall effect. Pastels are usually done on a coloured surface; the paper must also have some texture in order to hold the pigment (this is known as "tooth"). If you work on too smooth a surface, the pigment will tend to slip about and fall off, making it impossible to achieve any layering of colour in your picture.

PAPER AND TEXTURE SHADE

The reason for working on coloured paper is that it is very difficult, sometimes impossible, to cover the whole surface with pastel. Even if you use a pastel stick fairly heavily on its side, some of the paper will still show through. Small flecks of white paper appearing between pastel strokes create a jumpy effect, as well as devaluing the colours. Thus it is usual to work on a colour that either complements or tones in with the overall colour scheme of the picture. There are artists who like to work on white paper, but they are very much in the minority.

There are two standard papers made for pastel work: Ingres and Mi-Teintes (these are not manufacturers' names; they describe a type of paper). Both are made in a wide range of colours and both have a texture to hold the pigment in place. Ingres is a laid paper, with a pattern of fine, even lines, while Mi-Teintes has a pattern of dots slightly resembling fine chicken wire. It is worth trying both of these, as you will only discover which one you like best by hands-on experience. You can also use the "wrong" side of Mi-Teintes paper if you find the grain too obtrusive.

The choice of colour is more difficult, as it involves knowing what your picture will look like before you start. Some artists choose a paper which will be one of the key colours in the painting, and leave areas of it

1 AND 2 MI-TEINTES

3 AND 4 INGRES

5 SANDPAPER

6 AND 7 SANSFIX PAPER

8 WATERCOLOUR PAPER

FIXATIVE

Although some artists dislike fixative and use it as little as possible or even not at all, you will certainly need it when you are starting out in pastel. Unless you can frame and glaze your pictures immediately, there is a serious risk of smudging them if you fail to spray them with fixative before putting them away. Even after fixing, you will still need a sheet of tissue paper on top of the picture to protect it.

The problem with fixative is that it does tend to darken the colours slightly; you may also lose something of the delicate, fragile texture of pastel pigment. However, for any painting built up thickly in layers, it is essential to spray at regular stages, in order to overwork with new colours without disturbing earlier ones. Keep the spray as light as you can – several sparing applications are better than one heavy one – and don't continue working until you are sure the fixative is completely dry.

You can either use a bottle of fixative with a mouth diffuser or an aerosol can; the latter are all now "ozone friendly" and produce a suitably fine spray. They are quite expensive, however, so you might like to consider using odourless hairspray as an alternative – the ingredients are much the same.

SPRAY FIXATIVE

LIQUID FIXATIVE

MOUTH DIFFUSER

uncovered. For example, a blue-grey might be chosen for a landscape or seascape seen under a cloudy sky, with parts of the paper left for areas of sky and water. Other artists like to work on a contrasting colour, choosing, for example, yellow for a snow scene consisting mainly of blues and blue-greys. To start with, it is probably best to choose a neutral mid-toned colour such as light grey or beige; very bright or very dark colours are hard to manage until you know what you are doing.

OTHER PAPERS

You can also work on a variety of papers not actually designed for pastel work, such as medium (Not surface) watercolour paper (CP paper). This has a very pronounced texture, which breaks up the pastel strokes,

while also allowing for heavy build-ups of colour. If you use watercolour paper, you can tint it in advance by laying a watercolour wash. There are also three special papers produced for pastels, used by artists who like to build up colours very thickly: sandpaper, velour paper and Sansfix paper.

Sandpaper is the same as the fine sandpaper sold for carpentry and other work around the home, but the artist's version comes in much larger sheets. Velour paper, as its name implies, has a velvety texture and gives an attractive soft line. The third alternative, Sansfix (also called Rembrandt paper depending on who makes it), is similar to sandpaper but slightly less abrasive. There is no need for fixative when using any of these papers.

Pastel is a drawing medium as well as a painting one, in as much as the pastel stick, like a pencil, is the direct intermediary between your hand and the paper. Although it is possible to produce a pastel painting in which all the colours are smoothly blended and there are no visible lines or marks, this is something of a lost opportunity, as the way in which pastel bridges the gap between drawing and painting is one of its major attractions. In the 18th century, when pastel painting became very popular, artists such as Jean-Etienne Liotard and Maurice Quentin de La Tour produced works whose smooth finishes emulated contemporary oil paintings. However, nowadays most artists prefer to exploit the mark-making aspect of pastel, to give free rein to its energetic, linear quality.

In order to do this successfully, you will need to develop your own "handwriting" in pastel. The tip of a pastel stick can produce a wide variety of different marks, depending on the pressure you apply, the sharpness or bluntness of the point and how you hold the stick. To practise mark-making, don't try to draw actual objects, but just doodle or scribble as the mood takes you. Try applying heavy pressure at the start of a line and then tapering off towards the end, or twisting the stick in mid-stroke so that it trails off in a narrow tail.

Although pastel is soft and crumbly, you will find that you can make surprisingly fine lines if you break a stick in half and use the edge of the broken end. However, hard pastels are the ones for really crisp details, so if you have these in addition to soft pastels, experiment with them too.

SIDE STROKES

The way to cover large areas of the paper in pastel painting is to sweep the side of the stick across the paper, thus depositing a

(Below) *These swatches show the variety of marks that you can make with the tip and side of a pastel stick.*

G

P
A
S
T
E
L

P
A
I
N
T
I
N
G

MAUREEN
JORDAN
NUDE AGAINST
PINK

*A classic combination of
line and side strokes can
be seen in this lively
figure study. Notice
how the artist has used
the pastel sticks in a
descriptive way, follow-
ing the directions of the
shapes and forms.*

broad band of colour. Side strokes can,
however, be much more than just a means
of "blocking in" – they can be as varied,
beautiful and expressive as line strokes.
Many different effects can be created by
varying the pressure and direction of the
stroke, by laying one stroke over another,
by blending in some areas and by laying one
colour over another.

The length of the pastel stick also affects
the kind of stroke you make. Unless you are
using hard pastels, which are relatively
tough, you will nearly always have to break
the stick. If you try to make side strokes
with the whole length of the stick, it will
probably break under pressure anyway,
added to which a short length is more
controllable. Usually the length should not

be more than 5 cm (2 in), but you can use
much smaller pieces of pastel than these to
make short, jabbing strokes, similar to
linear marks.

The other factor which affects side
strokes, even more than linear ones, is the
texture of the paper. A heavy texture such
as watercolour paper will break up the
stroke, producing a grainy effect, with the
colour deposited only on the top of the
weave. On smoother paper, the colour will
be denser and, if you apply the pastel
heavily, it will cover the paper thoroughly.
Be warned that, if you intend to use side
strokes as a means of colour mixing, with
one colour laid over another, the pressure
should be kept light initially, or the paper
will quickly become clogged.

MIXING PASTELS

However many pastels you have – and professional pastel painters may have hundreds – you will nearly always have to mix them to reproduce the colours you see. Nature provides far more subtle and varied nuances of colour than could be matched by any manufacturer of artist's pigments.

LIGHTENING AND DARKENING COLOURS

As mentioned earlier, all pastel colours are made in light and dark versions. Further variations of tone (the lightness and darkness of colours) are produced by controlling the amount of pressure you apply to the pastel stick – the heavier the pressure, the more solid the colour will be. However, you will frequently have to lighten or darken colours by mixing. A pale blue sky, for example, may call for a combination of blue and white, or blue and pale grey; dark areas of foliage or heavy shadows may need a mixture of dark blue or black with green and other colours. Black is particularly useful in pastel work as the colours are brilliant and generally not very dark, so it is hard to achieve any depth of colour without using black.

METHODS OF MIXING

One of the best-known techniques for colour mixing is blending. Two or more colours are applied to the working surface and rubbed together with your fingers, a rag, a piece of cotton wool or an implement called a torchon (a rolled paper stump made specially for the purpose). If you choose your pastel sticks carefully, you can achieve almost any colour and tone in this way. However, although blending is ideal for areas of a picture where you want a soft effect, you should not rely on it too much, as over-blending gives a bland impression.

Lightening

1 *When very pale pastel colours are required, it is sometimes necessary to mix on the paper surface by adding white. Here white is laid over a mid-blue.*

2 *The pastel pigments are gently blended together with a finger-tip. Be prepared to use your fingers a good deal in pastel work; they are the best "implements" for blending in relatively small areas.*

Darkening

1 *Black is a useful colour in pastel work, as it can be difficult to achieve really dark colours without it. Here the black is laid down first, with the green on top.*

2 *With experience you will discover which colours can be successfully darkened with black. In this case, the mixture is rather muddy and the light green has lost much of its character.*

Mixing greens

To reproduce the wide range of greens in nature, you generally need to mix colours to some extent. Here, ultramarine is laid over a lemony yellow. The two colours are blended lightly to produce a strong green. Yellows and blues can also be added to ready-made greens to modify them.

Mixing oranges

To mix a pure orange, choose the strongest red and yellow in your pastel set, and lay the yellow over the red. Even when the two colours are blended, the darker colour will dominate if it is laid over the lighter one. Experiment to discover the effect of light-over-dark and dark-over-light mixtures.

Mixing greys

Most pastel ranges include a good selection of greys, but they can easily be mixed from black and white. Other colours, such as blues and greens, can be added for interest. The result will be affected by the order in which the colours are laid: white over black will produce a lighter mixture, particularly if the colours are only blended gently.

Blending large areas

1 *For a subtle blend which would be suitable for a large area of sky, blue and black are first lightly scribbled together.*

2 *The rag used to blend the colours knocks some of the particles of pastel off the paper, producing a lighter mixture than finger blending, which pushes the pigment into the paper.*

Feathering

This is a useful method for rejuvenating an area of colour which has become flat and dull, or for toning down an over-bright colour. Here light feathering strokes are made in green over an area of red.

A light, unblended application of one colour over another makes a more vibrant and exciting alternative because the first colour shows through the second, producing an attractive sparkle. Pastels are opaque, and so light colours can be laid over dark ones as well as the other way round, to modify the tone of colours.

For many artists, one of the main attractions of pastel is its vigorous linear quality, with the marks of the pastel stick forming an integral part of the image (like brushwork in painting). For this reason, colours are sometimes mixed by building up a network of linear strokes which merge when seen from a distance. A related method is feathering, which is often used to revive an area of colour which has become flat and dull through over-zealous blending. It involves dragging light strokes of colour over the offending area with the tip of the pastel stick and provides a useful means of modifying colours which do not look quite right. For example, a solid area of red which seems too bright in the overall context of your painting can be feathered over lightly with strokes of green, or a too-blue sky can be transformed with greys or pale mauves.

CHOOSING PAPER

When one colour is laid over another it produces a third colour – yellow over blue makes green; red over yellow makes orange and so on. Thus it follows that the colour of the paper will influence the applied colour. If you choose a neutral mid-toned paper the effect will not be dramatic, but a light application of yellow on a rich blue paper has a similar effect to laying yellow over blue pastel. It is important to remember this, as the paper always acts as a third colour in any two-colour mixture, unless the pastel is applied heavily. On the following pages you can see some of the effects of the paper colour on mixtures.

GEOFF MARSTERS
FEN LIGHT
(Above) *Rich painterly effects have been achieved by laying one colour over another, with the work fixed between stages. For the bright patches of highlight in the fields, the artist has used the tips of the pastel sticks, applying thick colour over softer blends.*

Using the paper colour

Overlays

(Above) *As you can see in these examples, even when pastel is applied thickly, small specks of the paper will show through, affecting the appearance of the applied colour. The colour of the paper also influences the way you work, acting as the "key" against which you must judge the first colours you put on. Working on black or very dark blue paper makes it difficult to assess the lighter colours, because even a brilliant green or red will look pale in comparison. Until you have gained some experience, it is wise to choose a mid-toned neutral colour, thus avoiding the possibility of the base colour working against you.*

(Left) *Thoroughly blended colour mixtures may be necessary in certain areas of a painting, but the effects of unblended colours are often more exciting. In these examples you can see how one colour shows through another to produce a lively, sparkling effect.*

EXERCISE: EXPERIMENTING WITH DIFFERENT PAPERS

It requires a good deal of experience to know which colour of paper to choose, so it is not a bad idea to start by painting the same subject on two different colours. Set up a simple still-life group, making sure that whatever objects you choose have a predominant colour theme. You might decide on blue, in which case you could paint a bunch of blue flowers, perhaps with one or two yellow ones for contrast. Or you might set up a still life consisting of green bottles, again with one other colour for contrast – perhaps an orange or apple.

Paint the still life first on a colour which is the opposite of the main colour in the group. This is orange-yellow if you have chosen blue as the predominant colour, and red or red-brown if you have decided on green. These opposite colours are called complementaries; there are three pairs of them: red and green, blue and orange, and yellow and violet. For your second painting, choose a paper which represents one of the colours in the subject. For the blue flower group you could use a dark or mid-toned blue, or a blue-grey. You should find that you don't have to cover the entire paper with pastel colour.

Some artists always use a complementary coloured paper, while others prefer one which tones with the key subject colour.

Painting on toning paper

1 *Working on dark green paper, chosen in order to represent the dominant greens of the still life, the artist begins with the opposite colour, making a light drawing in red-brown pastel.*

2 *Initially, she concentrates on covering the green paper in the non-green areas, establishing the contrasting warm browns and blue-whites. Notice that she does not attempt to cover the paper entirely; the paper colour still shows through.*

Painting on contrasting paper

1 *In this case the paper picks up the yellow-brown of the board, but is in opposition to the greens of the vegetables.*

2 *To counteract the colour of the paper, the artist has to use a different selection of greens and yellows from those she chose for the first painting. Here the colour scheme is warmer and the greens are also less dominant.*

3 *Leaving the paper colour to stand for the mid-tones of the vegetables, she now builds up both the dark shadows (the pepper in the background) and the brighter green highlights. Touches of the warm browns and yellows used for the chopping board have also been introduced into the vegetables, so that the green-brown theme runs through the picture.*

4 *The finished picture shows the importance of the role played by the colour of the paper. Large areas have been left uncovered on the vegetables; elsewhere in the painting, streaks and flecks of the green base colour show through the light pastel strokes. Repeating colours from one part of a picture in another area makes a series of visual links, creating an overall unity in the composition.*

3 *In the first painting, the greens of the vegetables were applied quite lightly because the paper did not need to be covered completely. Here, however, the greens have to be built up heavily to prevent too much of the paper from showing through.*

4 *There are a number of differences between this and the first painting. The dominant colour here is orange-brown rather than green, with the paper colour showing through most clearly on the board and in the background. The method of working has also been affected by the need to build up the greens heavily; the vegetables look darker and more solid, forming a stronger contrast with the wooden board. Both paintings are on the "wrong" – smoother – side of Mi-Teintes paper, chosen in preference to the more obtrusive texture of the "right" side.*

TINTING YOUR PAPER

The two standard pastel papers, Ingres and Mi-Teintes, are produced in a vast range of colours. However, some artists, particularly those who like to build up their colours thickly, prefer to work on watercolour paper, which has a distinctive texture, and which they generally tint in advance with their chosen colour.

LAYING A TINTED GROUND

There are two ways of doing this. One is by laying a wash, either of watercolour or thinned acrylic paint, which is quick and easy. However, if you work exclusively in pastel you won't have these paints to hand, in which case you can prepare the paper with what is called a dry wash of pastel. To do this you first reduce a pastel stick to dust by holding it over a bowl or plate and scraping the long edge with a sharp knife. When you have sufficient colour, simply dip a piece of cotton wool (a cotton ball) or a rag into it and spread it over the paper surface, using an even pressure.

If you want an all-over colour, spread the pastel dust evenly across the paper. This method also allows you to introduce tonal variations by applying the colour more thickly in some areas than others. You can also use more than one colour, perhaps using a blue dry wash for a sky in a land-scape and a brown or yellow ochre one for the ground. Indeed, dry washing need not be restricted to colouring the ground or sky, it is also a useful method for creating hazy effects of soft colour. If you intend to work over the wash, however, spray it with fixative first. The advantage of the water-colour or acrylic method is that you need not do this.

Laying a dry wash

1 *A knife is used to scrape the side of the pastel stick, producing a fine dust. The method may seem wasteful, but in fact you don't need a great deal of colour.*

2 *This dry wash is for a landscape, using two colours: blue for the sky and yellow for the land. The blue powder is applied lightly on watercolour paper with a piece of cotton wool (a cotton ball).*

3 *Some of the blue has been taken into the land area, and the yellow applied on top, so that the two colours overlap to produce a yellow-green mixture. Before starting the painting proper, the dry wash should be sprayed with fixative.*

Wet brushing with a bristle brush

1 *Working on watercolour paper, the artist began by sketching out the composition. Having blocked in the large areas with side strokes, she then used a pastel tip to sketch in the shapes of the trees.*

2 *A bristle brush dipped in water is used to spread the colour. This type of brush, being harder than a watercolour brush, creates a more thorough spread of colour, dislodging more particles.*

3 *She proceeds to draw over the wet-brushed areas with the tip of the pastel stick to add touches of crisp definition to the tree trunks and branches. In places, she has also drawn on still-damp paper to create softer lines and strokes.*

Wet brushing with a soft brush

Clean water taken over pastel marks with a soft brush releases some of the colour to form a watercolour effect, leaving the marks of the pastel stick intact. Watercolour paper rather than pastel paper should be used for this method, as the latter may buckle.

WET BRUSHING

If you go over soft pastel marks with a brush dipped in clean water, it releases some of the colour while leaving the pastel strokes clearly visible. You can use this technique only on watercolour paper, as the standard pastel papers are quite thin and would buckle under the water. If you like to work on watercolour paper, however, wet brushing forms a useful alternative to tinting the paper in advance. It allows you to cover the surface quickly with colour, obliterating the distracting white specks you see between strokes on white paper.

Wet brushing over side strokes produces a granular wash, which is ideal for suggesting the texture of objects such as rocks, cliffs or the barks of trees in a landscape. Over linear strokes, the effect is somewhat similar to that of line and wash in watercolour, with the wash a paler version of the original line. Wet brushing is often used to "pull together" lines and marks made with soft pastel or pastel pencil; it can also create light and shade effects to suggest form.

The idea of wetting pastel colour is not new. Edgar Degas, who took to pastel painting when his eyesight began to fail, was one of the greatest technical innovators in the medium. He would make a paste of his pastels, sometimes steaming his board or spraying warm water over the colours and then working into them with stiff brushes, before overlaying further linear marks.

UNDERPAINTING

The practice of working over an under-painting, usually done in either watercolour or acrylic, is rapidly gaining acceptance in pastel-painting circles. It stems from the same idea as colouring the paper in advance, but goes several steps further. By making a full-scale underpainting, you can introduce as many colours as you like before laying on any pastel, and so relate the colours to the shapes in your picture. Alternatively you can make a monochrome underpainting to establish the drawing and main tonal structure of the painting, perhaps choosing a colour which contrasts with the overall colour key of the subject.

The advantage of a multi-coloured underpainting is that you can carry out at least some of the colour mixing at the painting stage. This helps to avert one of the potential dangers of pastel painting: over-mixing and clogging the surface of the paper. You can also work on smoother paper than usual; as you will not be laying so many layers of pastel colour, there will be less risk of the pastel pigment slipping off the surface. As a general rule pastel paper should be textured, but it can be exciting to work on a smoother surface, such as Hot-pressed watercolour paper. This does not break up the pastel strokes as much as the medium-surface (Not, or CP) paper normally used for watercolour work, thus allowing you to lay thick, solid areas of smooth colour.

Pastel over paint

1 *Working on medium-surface watercolour paper, the artist begins with watercolour. He allows the brushmarks to show in order to complement the pastel strokes.*

2 *Light pastel marks now overlay the paint in the foliage and sky areas, and pale grey is used to draw into the darker blue-greys.*

3 *As he wishes to achieve a blend of the two media, the pastel colours chosen are close to those of the watercolour beneath. There is no attempt to cover the first colours completely.*

4 *The artist works from the centre of the picture outwards, and now lays down more watercolour, again using brushstrokes which suggest the movement of the foliage.*

5 *The railings have been reserved as highlights, with the watercolour painted around them and later light applications of grey pastel giving a suggestion of modelling. The central area of foliage is now darkened so that the whites stand out clearly.*

6 *(Above) Some artists use a watercolour underpainting much as they would a coloured ground, covering most of it with pastel. In this case, however, the two media work together, with the watercolour playing an important part in the overall effect.*

WET BRUSHING OIL PASTEL

Oil pastel is an exciting medium to use, although it is very different in character from soft pastel, being bound with oil rather than gum. Its dense, rather greasy quality means that it fills the grain of the paper relatively quickly, making it less suitable for colour mixing by layering.

However, this is only true if the medium is used "dry" like conventional pastel. The great advantage of oil pastel is that the colour can be melted with an application of turpentine or white spirit and spread with a brush or rag over the paper (with canvas or oil-sketching paper as possible alternatives). This allows you to lay broad areas of colour very quickly and you can then work over these with more linear strokes, building up the picture with a succession of wet and dry layers. If the paper becomes clogged, you can remove whole areas of colour by applying more turpentine and rubbing gently with a rag. On oil-sketching paper you can make as many such corrections as you like, without harming the surface.

Oil pastels come in a more limited colour range than soft pastels, but this wet-brushing method allows you to achieve very subtle colour mixes on the working surface. As with paints, you can even mix colours on a palette before putting them on. Simply moisten the tip of a pastel stick with a brush dipped in turpentine to release the colour and transfer this to the palette.

As oil pastels are quick to use, easy to correct and, best of all, do not need fixing they make an ideal medium for outdoor sketching. However, they do have a tendency to melt under a hot sun, becoming very soft and buttery, which makes them hard to manage; it is best to work in the shade wherever possible.

Oil pastel and white spirit

1 *Working on oil-sketching paper, the artist blocks in the composition lightly with very soft oil pastels. You can also work on ordinary pastel paper, such as Ingres, but there is a slight possibility of the oil in the pastels causing deterioration over time.*

2 *A bristle brush dipped in white spirit is used to spread and mix the colours. The mixture is relatively transparent because the first colours were applied lightly. If colour is built up too thickly in the early stages, mixtures can become muddy and dull.*

3 Further brushwork over the whole picture has now firmly established the form and colours of the trees. Again, you can see how the artist has avoided over-mixing and churning up the colours; blues and yellows can be clearly distinguished in the dark and light green areas.

4 The beauty of this method is that amendments can be made simply by wiping off colour with a rag, dipped in white spirit. The foreground needs to be softened, so the whole area is wiped down prior to re-working.

5 To produce a textured effect on the foliage, the artist works into a still-wet area with firm strokes of the pastel stick. This creates distinctive marks and slight ridges rather similar to the effects of sgraffito.

6 For colour contrast and a suggestion of the trunks and branches, dark red oil pastel is now used to draw over the earlier colours. The artist keeps the marks very broad and free; her approach is impressionistic.

7 As the pastel has been used in a series of thin washes, rather like glazing in oil painting, the colours are beautifully luminous, an effect enhanced by the white paper reflecting through the colours. When using oil pastel in this way, white paper can be a better choice than coloured.

CHARCOAL AND PASTEL

Charcoal and pastel are frequently used together; they are natural partners because both have a similar texture. As under-drawings for pastel work should never be done in pencil – the greasiness of graphite repels the pastel colour – charcoal is often used to make the preliminary line drawing. Any loose dust is then brushed away and the charcoal is fixed before the pastel colour is applied on top.

In this case the charcoal is largely obliterated by the overlaid colours and plays no part in the finished work. However, it can also be used in a more positive way, with the charcoal complementing the pastel colour. As charcoal gives a clearer, crisper line than soft pastel, it is sometimes used to define detail and provide a linear structure, with the pastel used for the broader colour areas (like line and wash in watercolour painting).

Another approach, sometimes used for figure work and portraiture, is to make a tonal underdrawing, using the side of the charcoal stick to establish light and dark areas. This is suitable only for paintings which are to be relatively "low-key" in colour, as, even when the charcoal is fixed, the pastel laid on top picks up a little of the black dust. This has the effect of muting the pastel colours, which can be very effective for certain subjects.

Charcoal can also be used hand in hand with pastel colours and, because it is less dense than black pastel, it is particularly useful for the subtle mid-toned colours which are often hard to mix successfully. The grey-greens or grey-blues seen in the middle distance of a landscape, for example, can often be achieved by mixing charcoal and green or blue pastel, or by dragging a light veil of charcoal over a pastel colour to tone it down.

Making a charcoal underdrawing

1 *The colour scheme planned for this picture is relatively sombre, with a predominance of dark tones, so the charcoal drawing is made on a mauve-blue paper chosen to set the key for the later colours. The paper is Mi-Teintes, used on the smoother side.*

2 *With the underdrawing complete, the excess charcoal dust is flicked off the paper with a bristle brush. The drawing is sprayed with fixative before the pastel colours are applied, so that the charcoal does not muddy the colours.*

3 *The artist's method is to build up her colours gradually with a series of overlays. The bright pink used for the sky at this stage will be modified by later applications. Although dark in tone, the colours chosen for the buildings are very rich.*

5 The highlights have been left until the final stage, because pastels are opaque and it is therefore possible to cover dark colours with light ones. Notice the variety of colours used for the walls of the houses, from deep greens to reds and pinks, plus a mauve produced by the paper colour showing through the original charcoal drawing.

4 The side of a short length of white pastel is now dragged lightly over the earlier pink; some of this is still visible, as is some of the paper colour. The sides of the buildings nearest to this sky area have also been lightened slightly.

6 Finishing touches have been added to define the details of the buildings with fine lines (made with the edge of a broken pastel stick), and to suggest the large tree behind the houses on the left. Both of the trees are important to the composition, but play a minor part, so they have been treated lightly, with smeared strokes, to merge them partially into the sky.

BUILDING UP PASTEL

Although the standard pastel papers are versatile and allow for a certain amount of layering, you cannot build up colours really thickly on them. For those who like truly painterly effects, it is worth trying one of the special papers produced for pastel painting: sandpaper, velour paper and Sansfix paper.

These papers handle very differently from the normal pastel paper. Sandpaper in particular grips the pastel pigment so firmly that it is virtually impossible to blend colours by spreading them with either your fingers or a rag; for the same reason you cannot move colours around on the surface. However, the paper's firm hold on the pastel pigment means that you can go on layering colours more or less indefinitely. This creates very subtle mixtures and great depth of colour as well as effects similar to that of impasto in oil painting, where the brushstrokes stand proud of the surface. In fact, some pastel paintings on sandpaper look very much like oil paintings.

These papers all have one disadvantage: they are very "greedy" with the pastel colours and you will get through your pastels at a faster rate than when working on Ingres or Mi-Teintes paper. This is partially balanced by the fact that you won't need much – if any – fixative, which is fairly expensive. If you find the paper beginning to clog you can use fixative, but it is not normally necessary. It is best not to fix the finished painting, as this will tend to darken the colours.

Working on Sansfix paper

1 *This paper grips the colour more firmly than the standard papers and is ideal for creating painterly effects in pastel. Here, the artist begins work on the lightest areas.*

2 *A solid line of black is now pulled down the paper to define the pole leaning against the windowsill, which provides a visual balance for the artist's easel.*

3 *The colours on the face and body have been built up more thickly, and both grey and yellow added to the original application of white on the window. The paper allows for a considerable amount of building up by such layering methods.*

4 *Using a small piece of pastel, the artist now lays light grey over the white. He has deliberately allowed small patches of the dark grey paper to show through to create a lively broken-colour effect.*

5 The finished picture, with its thick and heavy pastel marks, is reminiscent of an oil painting. This paper is not suited to very delicate approaches or to blending techniques.

LAYING A TEXTURED GROUND

The underlying texture of the paper is always an important factor in pastel paintings. Some artists like to work on a texture of their own making, rather than relying on the mechanically produced overall texture of the paper. A "home-made" texture can take any form you like, but the most usual one is a series of irregular diagonal or vertical brushstrokes, which give a directional emphasis to the overlaid pastel strokes. Such grounds can be laid with acrylic paint, used fairly thickly so that it holds the marks of the brush, with acrylic gesso, or, for a really heavy texture, with a substance called acrylic modelling paste, thinned with water. The latter is only sold in large pots, however, and is quite costly, so make sure you like this way of working before you invest in it.

The advantage of using acrylic paint is that you can colour the ground as well as texturing it. You can even combine the texture element with a coloured under-painting, varying the colours and textures from one area of the painting to another. Don't overdo it, however, as you don't want to introduce too many different elements before you even begin to apply the pastel. This method is best suited to thick applications of pastel; you will need to work on a tough paper, such as heavy watercolour paper – don't try to lay a ground on ordinary pastel paper, as it will buckle under the weight of the paint.

A tinted and textured ground

1 *Acrylic gesso, which is sold primarily for preparing boards and canvases for oil and acrylic painting, makes an excellent textured ground for pastel work. It is slightly thicker in consistency than tube acrylic and it dries fast. Here it has been mixed with black acrylic paint and applied to thick watercolour paper with a large bristle brush.*

2 *The deliberately uneven application of the ground creates a surface which will break up the pastel strokes in interesting ways. This gives an exciting element of unpredictability, allowing you to exploit semi-accidental effects.*

3 As colour is scribbled over the brushstrokes of acrylic gesso, it catches only on the raised areas, creating a series of strongly textured marks. This is a method which is best suited to broad, impressionistic approaches; with a heavy underlying texture it is not possible to achieve fine detail.

4 (Left) Here the artist uses broad strokes of pastel to capture the essential colours and shapes of the flowers.

5 (Above) As the pastel cannot completely cover the brushmarks of the gesso ground, in the final stages the artist turned to a painting method, dipping a brush into gesso and painting over the pastel. This mixed with and spread the colour, giving a broad painterly effect.

SGRAFFITO

This technique, in which one layer of colour is scratched or scraped into to reveal another one below, is sometimes used in oil painting. It is now also one of the recognized techniques in oil pastel, which is really oil paint in solid form. You can scratch into soft pastel, too, provided that you work on a tough surface, such as watercolour paper, and spray the first layer of colour with fixative before applying the second.

However, the effects are more dramatic and exciting in oil pastel and, because oil pastel colours cling to the surface very firmly and do not need fixing, they are tailor-made for the method. The effects that you can achieve are many and various, depending on the tool you use for the scratching, the amount of pressure you apply, the thickness of the colours and the

texture of the painting surface. For example, if you work on a fairly smooth paper which doesn't break up the pastel strokes, lay one colour thickly over another and then scratch into the top layer with a sharp point, you can make a fine, delicate line drawing. Working on a more heavily textured paper and scratching into a layer of colour with the side of a knife, on the other hand, will give a broader, more generalized effect of broken colour, as the knife will remove only some of the colour. You can work either dark over light or light over dark, building up several different layers of colour then scratching into each one in turn; alternatively you can vary the colour combinations from one part of the picture to another – the possibilities of this technique are endless.

Sgraffito landscape

1 *Working on heavy watercolour paper, the artist has laid a foundation of light, bright colours which she will partially reveal by scratching back later colours with a knife or scalpel.*

2 (Right) *Dark greens, blues and red-browns have now been laid over the first colours, and a knife used to scratch into the central area and the tree at top left. To reinforce the broken-colour effect, much of the yellow has been left showing between strokes of green. This gives added vibrancy.*

3 *Heavy diagonal strokes of deep blue are now laid over the green area in a loose cross-hatching technique. The pastel marks follow the same direction as the earlier scratch marks in order to integrate the sgraffito technique fully into the picture.*

4 *With the point of a loosely held scalpel, the artist lightly scribbles into the layers of oil pastel. There is now a considerable build-up of different colours, and the scratching reveals brilliant blues and greens as well as the original yellow.*

5 *Although the technique is most often associated with fine lines, broader effects can also be achieved; here, the side of a palette knife is pulled down the tree trunk. The palette knife has also been used to remove parts of the top colour in the foreground beneath the trees to suggest patches of strong sunlight filtering through the leaves.*

6 *(Above) The successive layers of scraped-back colour combined with the vigorous pastel marks create a lovely effect of shimmering light. The sgraffito has been carefully handled so that its effects are neither over-obtrusive nor self-conscious; this technique should never be allowed to dominate.*

COMPARATIVE DEMONSTRATION

If you visit an exhibition of pastel paintings you may well notice an amazing diversity of styles, even when the subject matter is similar. Three pastel landscapes by different artists, for instance, would probably bear little resemblance to each other, except in the medium used. Too often, amateur painters feel that there is a definite set of rules which must be followed, but, although hints can be given, there is really no right and wrong way of doing things. It is,

instead, up to each person to develop their own methods and artistic "handwriting". To demonstrate this, we have asked three artists to paint the same simple subject. The first, Patrick Cullen, whose work is shown on these pages, paints on watercolour paper. Debra Manifold, the second artist, works in oil pastel on oil-sketching paper, while Hazel Harrison uses standard pastels and a more conventional surface – Mi-Teintes paper.

Pastel on watercolour paper

1 *The artist began by laying a light watercolour wash to tone down the white of the paper and make it easier to assess the first colours. When the wash was dry, he made a careful charcoal drawing.*

2 *(Above right) His method of working is unusual: instead of laying down broad areas of colour at the outset and modifying them later, he proceeds methodically across the picture, treating each area separately. He is now completing the tablecloth, which will provide a context for the other colours.*

3 *(Right) To link the tablecloth to the bottom of the windowframe, which was painted next, the same grey was used. The cup and saucer provide the warmest colour area; the artist begins work here by defining the ellipse at the top and then blending the colours with his thumb.*

4 *The highlights on the saucer, like the ellipse on the top of the cup, define its shape, so they have been drawn in firmly in white. Few highlights are pure white, however, so they are now modified with light strokes of brown laid on top.*

5 *Although the tablecloth was more or less complete in the earlier stages, there was insufficient contrast between the shadowed area below the cup and this right hand side where the light falls. This is now lightened with pure white.*

6 (Below) *In spite of the simplicity of the subject and the limited colour scheme, the picture is satisfying and well-balanced, with the dark shapes of the window and the boxes on the left making a frame for the cup and saucer.*

Continued ▷

Oil pastel and white spirit

2 (Right) *The colours have been built up, and a brush dipped in white spirit is used to blend them. In order to balance the warm pinks and browns of the cup, similar colours have been introduced into the background.*

1 (Above) *The artist begins with a rough drawing in grey oil pastel and then applies light veils of colour with the side of the stick. Her drawing need not be as detailed as that of the previous artist because oil pastel can so easily be corrected.*

3 *This artist is always more concerned with the colour relationships in her painting than with the actual colours of the subject; here she chooses a vivid blue to contrast with the cup and saucer.*

4 *Having mapped out the grid of squares for the tablecloth, she now scribbles white pastel lightly over the blue, using diagonal strokes which blur and soften the lines to avoid too precise an effect.*

5 *The painting, with its vivid array of colours in the background and greenish blue in the foreground, is quite unlike the previous artist's interpretation. The style is very different too; the tablecloth has been treated in a much broader way and plays a less important role in the composition.*

1 *A dark blue paper has been chosen to pick up the colour of the tablecloth. Working on the smooth side, the artist has begun with a charcoal drawing.*

2 *The cup and saucer are seen as the key colour area, so she concentrates on this, finding it easier to assess the colours in the subject when working on a contrasting paper.*

3 *At this stage it becomes apparent that the perspective of the tablecloth is wrong, so the whole area is wiped down with a rag. Pastel cannot be erased completely, but removing the loose pigment makes it possible to over-work.*

4 *A ruler and white pastel pencil are now used to re-draw the grid of squares. Straight lines are not easy to draw, and rulers can save a lot of frustration.*

5 *(Above) The artist changes the composition from a horizontal to a vertical format by placing masking tape around the central area. The ellipse of the cup is then re-defined with white pastel. Finally, the artist lightly sketches a grid of squares on the window to echo the tablecloth and introduces some touches of mauve-blue into the background.*

LANDSCAPE

Both soft pastels and oil pastels are ideal for landscape work. The range of marks that you can make – from soft blends and sweeping strokes made with the side of the stick to sharp, linear marks – is capable of matching virtually any effect seen in nature. Both types of pastel are quick to use, allowing you to build up areas of colour very rapidly, and are perfect for capturing fleeting effects of weather and light.

Best of all, if you are working outside directly from the subject, you will need far less equipment than you would with paints. The only basic requirements are your box of pastels, some paper and a drawing board. However, there are one or two other items that you may find useful.

Landscape in close-up
(Left) *One of the most difficult decisions to make when faced with a large expanse of countryside is how much to include and what to focus on. You can often make a more expressive statement by moving in close, as Doug Dawson has done in* The Edge of the Meadow. *The strong diagonal thrust of the tree across the picture is balanced by the horizontal bands of colour formed by the foreground and by the light field in the middle distance.*

Tonal contrast

(Right) *A common cause of failure in landscape paintings is lack of attention to tones – the relative lightness and darkness of colours. In James Crittenden's* Spanish Landscape *the contrasts of tone not only convey the heat and strong sunlight, but also create a pattern of light and dark which gives a structure to the composition.*

Placing the horizon

(Opposite) *In a wide, panoramic landscape it is important to consider how to divide up the picture space, and how much prominence to give to the sky. The area of England in which Geoff Marsters works is very flat, with the great expanse of sky one of its most noticeable features, so in* Fen Landscape *he has given it three-quarters of the picture.*

Varying the greens

(Above) *Landscapes are frequently spoiled by poor observation of colours, particularly greens. Greens are extraordinarily varied, and you must further take into account the many nuances caused by light and shade. In Patrick Cullen's* Chickens, Petrognano, *the "greens" vary from silver-greys and creamy yellows to near-browns.*

If you work on a large scale using soft pastel you may need to invest in a portable sketching easel. You will quickly be covered in pastel dust if you try to work with your board propped on your lap, and an additional advantage of an easel is that you can step back from your painting periodically to assess it.

You will get your hands dirty whether you use an easel or not, so take some rags or, better still, a packet of moistened hand wipes. For oil pastel you will need white spirit and rags to clean your hands, plus brushes if you intend to spread the colours. You will not need fixative for oil pastels but you will do for soft pastels, as it is easy to smudge unfixed, finished work when you are carrying it home.

PLANNING IN ADVANCE

Even though time is usually limited when you are painting on the spot, it always pays to do some initial planning: choosing the best viewpoint, deciding how much of the scene in front of you to include in the picture and considering where to place the horizon. There is a natural tendency to divide the picture into two distinct areas of sky and land. This is not usually the best approach, however, particularly if it creates a central division – over-symmetry should always be avoided as it makes pictures look both dull and disjointed.

Give particular consideration to skies which are vitally important in landscape; not only are they the primary light source, they also play a major role in creating space. In a wide, panoramic landscape, for example, you can often increase the sense of depth and space by letting the sky occupy more of the picture area than the land – perhaps three-quarters of it. Conversely, with a mountain scene in which you want to express the upward thrust of the land, you could give minimum space to the sky.

Foregrounds are another important area – a painting can be easily spoiled by a weak or over-dominant foreground. As a general

Mark-making

(Above) *The marks you make with your pastel sticks are as important as brushstrokes in an oil painting. As well as helping to describe the forms, they add an extra dimension to the picture, giving it a life and movement of its own independent of the subject it represents. In James Crittenden's* Looking through the Blue Trees, *short directional strokes play a practical role in describing the leaves of the trees, but even in the foreground shadow individual marks are visible, "lifting" an area which might have become dull if treated in a flat way.*

rule, foregrounds should "introduce" the rest of the picture and lead the eye into it. Too much detail or very strong shapes in the foreground can sometimes have the opposite effect, acting as a block, or a closed door rather than an open one. You can often solve the foreground problem in advance by choosing the best position from which to work – how much of the foreground you see is directly related to whether your viewpoint is high or low. If you look at a scene first standing and then sitting down, you will notice how it changes completely. In a flat landscape, particularly, some feature in the foreground which you may have scarcely noticed suddenly becomes dominant, while objects in the middle distance are diminished in importance. There is no reason why you should not choose a low viewpoint – for a subject such as mountains it could be ideal – but it is often better to stand at an easel to paint, or to find a vantage point such as a low wall.

MAKING CHANGES

As pastels are opaque and one colour covers another quite easily, you can often change the composition in the early stages, perhaps by lowering a horizon or generally moving things around. However, it is a good idea to

guard against possible failure by taking a larger piece of paper than you think you will need and letting the composition grow as you work. Leave generous margins around the edges so that you can expand the picture at the top, bottom or sides if you need to – this is one of the many advantages of painting in pastel.

You can also make changes to the composition afterwards by cropping, a device often used by photographers to work out which area of a negative to print. When you re-assess your work a day or two later indoors, you may feel that it is not entirely satisfactory, although you are not sure why. Usually it is a compositional problem: for example, you may have placed some feature too centrally or included too much sky. If you cut four "corners" of thick paper or cardboard and move them around on the picture, you will be able to visualize possible improvements. A small change such as taking an inch or two off the foreground on one side can change the whole feel of the picture and bring it to life. Some artists do not bother over-much about composition when they are working on location, but do it all afterwards by cropping. Don't actually cut the painting, though – just make a mount (matt) which covers the unwanted areas.

Painting water

(Opposite) *Water is one of the most attractive painting subjects, but it is not as easy to paint as it seems. Although many different colours and tones can be discerned, particularly in reflections, they must be carefully controlled. In Jackie Simmonds's* Waterlilies and Reeds *the strongest contrasts of tone are those between the lilies and the foreground water – a deep, rich blue reflected from the sky.*

A focus for the eye

(Right) *Not all landscape paintings have an obvious centre of interest, or focal point, but often you will find that you are drawn to a particular view because of some dominant feature. In James Crittenden's* Almond Blossom in the Evening *the focal point is the pale tree, and he has drawn attention to it by using dark neutral colours for the hills beyond. To balance the light tone of the tree, he has introduced strong highlights on the grass on the left of the picture.*

Preliminary sketches

(Left) *Some landscape painters always work out of doors directly from their subject, taking the composition as they find it, while others prefer to compose their paintings in the studio from sketches, notes and sometimes photographs. Patrick Cullen's* Landscape in Le Crete *is a sketch for a very large-scale watercolour painting, which would have been impossible to complete on the spot. The directness of pastel makes it an ideal sketching medium.*

WORKING INDOORS

As it can be so difficult to compose paintings in front of the subject, a traditional way of working is to make a sketch or a series of sketches on the spot and compose the actual painting indoors. Often something you haven't quite pulled off can become the basis for a successful composition, so never throw away sketches, even if you are not happy with them. Working indoors removes some of the pressure, giving you the opportunity to think about how best to plan the painting, mix the colours and use the range of pastel marks in the context of the picture. Like brushstrokes in an oil painting, pastel marks are an important ingredient in composition; they are not just an "extra". Vigour and movement in a landscape painting can be conveyed by varying your strokes to include, perhaps, some sweeping directional side strokes, juxtaposed with more linear marks, short jabs and calligraphic squiggles (made with the tip of the pastel).

DEMONSTRATION

Artist Patrick Cullen specializes in landscapes, particularly the scenery of Tuscany, the subject of this painting. He works in oil and watercolour as well as pastel, usually on a large scale, composing his paintings in the studio from sketch references made on the spot. This pastel painting on sandpaper was done from colour sketches and a large charcoal "working drawing" in which he planned the composition.

1 *Referring to his charcoal drawing, which is the same size as the painting, the artist begins by mapping out the composition in pastel pencil. He works carefully, as it is impossible to erase pastel marks on sandpaper.*

2 *Sandpaper is unlike the standard pastel papers in that colours cannot be moved around to any great extent on the surface. Consequently, the artist works on each section of the picture separately, beginning with the mountains in the centre.*

3 *To create the textured effect of the foliage, he pushes his thumb into the pastel colour and twists it. He uses his fingers a good deal in the course of a painting.*

4 *The marks made by the pastel sticks are as important as brushwork in an oil painting; here you can see a wide variety of different strokes, from short jabs to tapering side strokes and crisp linear marks. These impart a lively energy to the picture as well as suggesting shapes and textures.*

5 *This illustration clearly shows the artist's method of working from the centre outwards. This piece-by-piece approach is unusual and is not recommended for beginners, as it involves having a clear vision of how the finished picture will look.*

6 *The edge of a broken pastel stick is used to make short, jabbing marks, contrasting with the long sweeping strokes elsewhere. Notice how the paper shows through between strokes, contributing to the overall colour effect.*

Continued ▷

7 *Leaving the sky until a late stage enables the artist to assess it in the context of the whole painting. He chooses yellows and pale blue-greys which echo the colours of the mountains. A bristle brush is used to blend the colours together slightly.*

8 *Further pale colours have now been dragged lightly over the original ones in the sky area, and the house is drawn with the tip of a pastel stick. Although small, the building is important to the composition because it provides a focus for the eye; you can see this in the finished painting.*

9 *On the right-hand side of the painting, the area above the white trees is developed with short strokes of green and yellow, following different directions to create a sense of movement.*

10 *The painting is now nearing completion, but requires some crisp touches and bright colours in the foreground to bring it forward in space. Vivid green is used both to suggest leaves and to outline some of the branches.*

11 (Right) *Again the artist exploits the contrast between hard and soft edges, now using the side of a short length of pastel to drag colour lightly above and around the branches.*

12 (Below) *Although the painting was virtually completed in one working session, the artist re-assessed it a day or two later and made some adjustments. The most significant of these was to increase the height of the trees on the right so that the white branches lead the eye in towards the dark tree-clad crevice, thus creating a visual link between foreground and distance.*

FLOWERS

When you open a new box of pastels you see an array of brilliant colours which suggests flowers, even before you have begun to put them on the paper. The soft, velvety textures also seem to emulate many of those seen in nature.

DRAWING

Flowers are certainly a wonderful subject and there are few pastel painters who have not at some time tried their hand at them. But, of course, there are problems – there always are. One of the most serious is that flowers are quite complex in shape and structure, both individually and *en masse* in an indoor arrangement and, therefore, you need to concentrate on the drawing. In a vase of flowers, for example, where there are many different shapes and colours as well as the vase itself, it is easy to go wrong and produce a painting in which the flowers and stems don't seem to relate to the container, or the flowerheads to the stems. In a watercolour or oil painting you can make a drawing in pencil first, erasing until you are sure you have it right, but you can't do this in pastel as the colour won't cover pencil marks.

You can, however, draw lightly in charcoal or in pastel pencil; the latter may be preferable in some cases as the charcoal could pollute the pastel colours. When working on coloured paper, choose a light-coloured pastel pencil for the drawing, or one that tones in with the overall colour scheme, and keep the drawing as simple as possible. If you are painting flowers in a vase, don't try to draw each individual bloom and stem; look for the overall shape made by the group.

Once you start to lay on the pastel colour, keep it light initially, as you will certainly find you have to change and redefine some

of the shapes. Try to build up the painting in large blocks of colour, leaving the details until last. It is difficult to achieve a high degree of detail with soft pastels, and pastel pencils or hard pastels may be helpful, when you come to the final stages. Meticulous attention to detail sometimes proves unnecessary anyway; pastel is essentially a medium for broad effects and it is often enough just to crispen the edge of a leaf or stem, here and there.

PATTERN

Flowers have an innate pattern element, hence their extensive use as motifs in all the applied arts, from embroidery and printed fabric to ceramics and china. Flowers in a

Unity through technique
(Above) *Pip Carpenter has carried the shapes of the flowers and leaves through into the background by using the same kind of strokes for both. This sets up a lively pattern all over the picture surface which enhances the feeling of movement. Jackie Simmonds has used a different technique in her still life* (opposite, above), *linking various elements by repeating colours.*

Unity through colour

(Below) *Although a large mixed bunch of flowers makes an attractive display, it is not always easy to tackle in a painting, as too many colours tend to fight with each other. It is often advisable to set up a group which has one dominant colour, as Jackie Simmonds has done in* Blue Marbles. *To maintain the coherence of the composition, she has repeated the deep blue of the marbles in various places on both of the pots, and has introduced blue into the background.*

Avoiding overworking

(Above) *The essence of flowers is freshness, and overworked or clogged colour can quickly destroy the impression. In* Orange Lilies, *Maureen Jordan has avoided the necessity of a heavy build-up of pastel by working on an acrylic underpainting. This has allowed her to establish the main colours with thin washes of paint, over which she has worked crisp, linear pastel strokes which beautifully describe the convoluted shapes of the petals.*

Flowers in landscape

(Left) *When flowers form only one element in a picture they usually need to be treated more broadly and simply than they would in an indoor group. The important features are the overall colour and the growth habit of the flowers. In* Bluebells at Isabella *by Maureen Jordan there is very little detail; even the flowers in the foreground are no more than small dots and dashes of pastel, yet they are immediately recognizable to anyone who has seen a bluebell wood.*

Light on dark

(Left) *A traditional way of painting white or light-coloured flowers is to set them against a dark background, which allows the artist to make the most of their delicacy and subtle nuances of colour. In* Jokers by the Pond, *Maureen Jordan has used the same idea but in an outdoor setting, with the sun and shade providing both excellent definition and contrasts of tone.*

vase create a pattern through the interaction of the various shapes and colours; you can stress this in your painting in a variety of ways. Attention can be drawn to the colour and pattern of an elaborate floral arrangement by setting it against a plain backdrop, perhaps even working on dark-coloured paper and leaving it uncovered in some areas. Alternatively, you can carry the pattern element right through the painting, choosing a decorated container for the flowers, and setting them against a wallpaper or some draped fabric with its own patterns and textures.

The way in which you use the pastel is also important in this context. You can create pattern as well as a sense of movement by letting the pastel strokes show in an active and positive way, rather than blending colours together. You might use strong, directional strokes for leaves and stems and, in the background, let the pastel stick follow the direction of the flowers to create a network of curving or vertical lines in different colours. As flowers are soft and delicate, there is always a tendency to over-blend, but bear in mind that this is not always the best approach.

Light on light

(Above) *An alternative approach for white or pale flowers is to set them against a white background and exploit the tonal contrasts in the flowers themselves, as Pip Carpenter has done in* White Daffodils. *Although the vase and the stems are the only genuinely dark areas, she has cleverly made use of shadows on the petals and subtle contrasts in the background, and has also played up the foreground shadow to balance the dark vase. It is surprising how many dark and middle tones can be seen in white.*

Complementary colours

(Above) *The colours opposite one another on a colour wheel – red and green, yellow and violet, orange and blue – are called complementaries, and they play an important part in painting as they set up exciting contrasts when used together. In Jackie Simmonds's* Tuscany Steps, *the red and green complementary pair was built into the subject, but she has also used yellow/ violet contrasts for both the plant pots and the steps to create areas of vibrant colour.*

HABITAT

Although the phrase "flower painting" tends to conjure up images of indoor arrangements, flowers in their natural setting can also make a rewarding subject. Whether it be garden flowers or wild flowers in a field, woodland or a patch of urban wasteland, the choice is yours. You cannot, of course, control the set-up or plan the colour scheme in advance, but you have a wide range of options with regard to composition and general approach.

Flowers in a garden or field, for example, could be treated as broad masses of colour or as colour accents in a landscape; alternatively, if you are interested in the shapes and colours of individual flowers, you could focus in more closely, making one or two blooms the subject of your painting. If you decide to make outdoor "portraits" of flowers, you must be aware of possible changes in the light but, as pastel allows you to build up colour effects very quickly, the problem is less acute than it might be in watercolour or oil painting.

Finally, don't ignore the fact that trees have flowers too; few subjects have more appeal than an orchard or a single blossom tree in spring. Here too you could take a close-up view and paint a single bough of blossom – the Oriental painters loved such effects. Trees with large and well-shaped flowers, such as magnolia, are particularly well-suited to this kind of treatment.

DEMONSTRATION

Rosalind Cuthbert works in a number of different media and subject areas – flowers are one of her interests, but she also paints portraits and landscapes. Her light and delicate pastel style is well suited to this elegant and colourful arrangement of tall flowers. She is working on smooth-surfaced watercolour paper, which she prefers to the medium-textured paper because it does not break up the strokes to the same extent, thus allowing for clear, crisp lines.

1 *The paper has been tinted using the dry-wash method. Yellow is the dominant colour in the painting, so the artist has chosen a deep yellow for the ground. She now draws the main shapes lightly in charcoal.*

2 *Having sketched in the leaves lightly with linear strokes of blue, she now draws the outlines of the two pink-and-white lilies with the tip of the pastel stick. Her method is to build up colours with a series of light overlays; the blue leaves will be modified later using other colours.*

3 (Right) *It is important not only to define the shape of the vase at an early stage but also to establish a balance of light and dark colours. In this area she works with the tip of the pastel, although some light side strokes can be seen in the background, where softer effects are needed.*

4 *These dark leaves play an important part in the picture, as the light–dark contrast between them and the flowerheads draws the eye to this central area.*

5 *(Right) The painting has now reached approximately halfway stage, with all the colours blocked in. The artist has been careful to work lightly and loosely to allow for later applications of colour and refinements of detail.*

6 *The foreground, which had been left relatively undefined, is now sharpened up with a crisp drawing of the piece of crumpled wrapping.*

7 *The frilly-edged petals of these carnations are suggested by linear marks drawn with a darker version of the original pink.*

Continued ▷

8 *The original blue used for the leaves has been overlaid with other colours and blended slightly to imitate their smooth texture. The pale grey, here used thickly for the highlights, also appears on the vase.*

9 *The dominant colour, yellow, is carried right through the painting, appearing in a paler version in both background and foreground. The pale grey background allows these small flowers to stand out, but they are treated lightly because the central flowers are the main focus for the eye.*

10 *The colours of the vase were too smoothly blended and were losing their liveliness and freshness, so small linear strokes are laid on top. This treatment has also set up a relationship between the vase and the leaves above.*

13 *(Opposite) Painting a group of tall flowers can cause problems of composition unless there is something in the foreground to create interest and to balance the shape of the vase. The artist has solved this by using the table top and the shape made by the wrapping paper as positive elements. The background, although lightly treated, is also carefully contrived, with the grey and red shapes at either side both balancing and enclosing the flowers and vase.*

11 *The flowers have been built up with layers of colour and occasional soft outlines, some made with hard pastel. A soft deep yellow pastel is now used to work carefully within the paler yellow edges of the petals.*

12 *A stick of hard pastel has been used to create a series of little broken lines on the petals of the pink-and-white lily. The underside is now toned down with grey, which mixes with the underlying pink to form a delicate mauve.*

P
A
S
T
E
L

P
A
I
N
T
I
N
G

121

FACES & FIGURES

Pastel seems tailor-made for portraits and figure paintings because of the way in which it doubles as a drawing and a painting medium. The range and versatility of pastel enables you to build up forms with broad areas of colour as well as to exploit different kinds of lines and marks. It is also suited both to full-scale finished compositions and to quick sketches.

PORTRAITS

Pastel has been a favoured medium for portraiture since the 18th century, when artists such as Rosalba Carriera and Maurice Quentin de La Tour became fascinated by its capacity for creating soft and delicate effects. Many of today's artists also find it an excellent medium for faces and figures, though the current emphasis is less on the subtle blending of colour than on the expressive quality of pastel marks.

Embarking on a portrait in pastel does require a degree of skill and confidence, as major changes cannot be made. If you find

Using the paper colour
(Right) *In portraiture and figure work it is particularly important to choose the right colour of paper, especially if you intend to leave areas of it uncovered, as in Ken Paine's superb* Young Girl. *The painting is almost monochromatic, with the lights and darks built up from the mid-tone of the brown paper.*

Light and mood
(Left) *For a portrait or figure painting in which it is important to describe features and forms accurately, it is best to choose side or three-quarter lighting, but backlighting can create lovely effects, silhouetting the figure, softening the colours and reducing the tonal contrasts. In his lovely* Mother and Child *Geoff Marsters has exploited this kind of lighting to create a gentle and meditative mood that is entirely in keeping with the subject.*

that you have misunderstood the shape and proportion of your subject's features, there is not, unfortunately, a great deal you can do about it. There are, however, some methods that you may find helpful initially, one of these being to work over a tonal underdrawing in charcoal. You can make as many changes as you like to the charcoal drawing because charcoal is easy to rub off and re-apply. Once you are happy with the drawing, you can spray it with fixative and apply the pastel colour on top.

Working on one of the pastel papers which allows you to make corrections by laying one colour over another may also boost your confidence. You can do this to some extent on any paper, but with Sansfix paper or sandpaper you can make quite major alterations.

PRACTISING PORTRAITURE

One of the difficulties with portrait painting is finding someone who is willing to sit for

Painting flesh tones

(Below) *In* Seated Nude *Robert Maxwell Wood has also chosen the paper wisely; it is almost the same colour as the mid-tone of the model's flesh, allowing him to use the pastel lightly and delicately. He has used blending methods in places, but has avoided over-doing this, as it can make the image appear bland and dull. Instead he has contrasted soft blends with crisp diagonal hatching lines and fine outlines made with the tip of the pastel to describe the fall of light on the head, neck and arms.*

Dramatic light

(Left) *Maureen Jordan has called her painting In the Spotlight and, as the title implies, the main subject is light rather than the figure itself, which is treated as a bold, broad generalization. She has applied the pastel thickly, working on textured watercolour paper, which allows a considerable build-up of pigment.*

you and who won't be insulted by early and possibly inept attempts! You always have one model on hand, however – yourself. Most artists have painted and drawn self-portraits at times during their careers; this is an excellent way of gaining practice in handling the medium, as well as acquiring confidence in the basic skills of portraiture.

Another good way of learning is to copy another artist's work; up until the end of the 19th century most artists considered this an essential part of their education. It is best to make what are known as "transcriptions", which means choosing a work in another medium, such as oils, as your model. If you try to make a faithful copy of someone else's pastel portrait, it will hinder the development of your own style, added to which, colour mixing will create additional problems because you are unlikely to have the same palette of colours.

You can also learn a lot about composition by copying. Do not only concentrate on trying to reproduce the forms and colours accurately; ask yourself why the artist has arranged the picture in a particular way. You might try making small pencil sketches from several different portraits, which will give you ideas about types of portrait composition. Some portraits, for example, show the whole

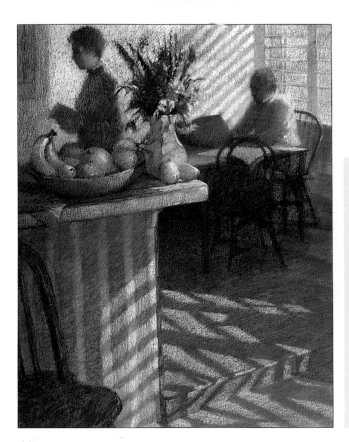

SKETCHING

Although you can sharpen your technical skills and learn to analyse composition by copying, the best practice of all is gained by drawing – as much and as often as possible. If you are drawing people purely for practice, you can use any medium with which you feel comfortable; but sketching has another purpose too: a series of colour sketches made in pastel can give you a good basis for a finished portrait or figure study. Many portraits are carried out from sketches, sometimes with the aid of a photograph to provide more detailed visual information.

Interiors with figures
(Above) *If you are painting a portrait, the face or figure will be the main centre of attention, with other elements such as furniture playing a subsidiary role, but in Sally Strand's* Passing Quietly *the figures are fully integrated into the interior of the room. The real subject of the painting is light and colour, and the people have been treated almost as inanimate objects, echoing the still life on the counter and the chair in the corner.*

figure, standing or seated; other show half or three-quarters of the body including the hands, while many "crop" just below the neck to show only the head and shoulders.

FIGURES IN A SETTING
Figure painting and portrait painting are closely linked, but there is one essential difference. The dictionary definition of a portrait is a "likeness of an individual", while a figure painting, whether it be a nude study or a group of figures in an indoor or outdoor setting, need not necessarily perform this function. This is not to say that the figures should be unrecognizable as individuals. Just as you would want a tree in a landscape to look different from its neighbour, some characteristic of a person should be stressed, but this need not be features – it can be posture, general shape or even the colour of clothing. You might

include a figure in a landscape, for example, simply because you want a bright accent of colour, or you might like the stark contrast of tone provided by a dark-clad figure in front of a sunlit whitewashed wall, in a Mediterranean town or village.

There are many reasons for drawing and painting figures other than portraiture, and the human element can be used, not as the whole subject of the painting, but as part of its visual "furniture". This is where the value of sketching really becomes apparent. People never remain in one place for long and you can seldom paint on the spot a landscape or townscape containing figures; such paintings are usually composed from sketches. Photographs are also a useful aid – don't become too reliant on them, but don't under-estimate their value either. Walter Sickert painted many urban scenes and figure compositions from photographs.

Composing the picture

(Right) *Even when you paint a head-and-shoulders portrait you need to consider how to place it on the paper and, in a full-length study, good composition is vitally important. In Maureen Jordan's* Amanda *the figure and sofa arm form a rough triangle, with the slope of the upper body balanced by the opposing line of the thigh. She has given only a hint of definition to the feet, allowing them to "bleed" out of the frame at the bottom so that the viewer's attention is focused on the face and body.*

Figure groups

(Below) *In landscape painting, a distant figure or group of figures is often introduced as a colour accent or an additional focus for the eye, but where figures form the whole subject, as in Sally Strand's charming* Crab Catch, *it is necessary to find ways of relating them to one another. Like many such compositions, this has an element of story-telling, with the boys sharing a common interest, but the artist has also used clever pictorial devices, notably the shapes and colours of the towel and bucket, to create a strong link between the two figures.*

INDEX

A
accurate drawing, 38-9
acrylic gesso, 98-9
animals, 56-9

B
balance lines, figures,
    48-51
Baptist, Gerry, 11, 47, 53
Bartlett, Paul, 10, 11, 52,
    62
blending pastels, 82-4
brush drawing, 26-7
brushes, 15
buildings, 60-7
burnishing, 30, 31

C
Cains, Gerald, 63
Carpenter, Pip, 8, 13, 75,
    114, 116
Carriera, Rosalba, 122
charcoal, 15, 18-19, 94-5
clothing, 52-3
coloured inks, 34-5
coloured pencils, 28-9,
    30-1, 36-7, 58-9
colours: drawing materials,
    28-9
 papers, 78-9, 84, 85, 86-7
 pastels, 76-7, 82-4
composition, 108, 123-4
Constable, John, 26
Conté crayons, 14-15, 20-1
contours, 45
Crittenden, James, 70, 75,
    107, 108, 109
cross-hatching, 16, 23, 30

Crowther, Stephen, 46
Cullen, Patrick, 71, 73,
    102-3, 107, 109,
    110-13
Cuthbert, David, 10, 47,
    53, 62
Cuthbert, Rosalind, 118-21

D
darkening pastels, 82
Dawson, Doug, 106
Degas, Edgar, 89
dry washes, 88

E
edge qualities, 44
Elliott Bates, Joan, 13
erasers, putty, 19
Evans, Ray, 63

F
feathering, pastels, 84
felt-tipped pens, 29, 34
figures, 39, 48-55, 124-5
fixatives, 78, 96
flowers, 114-21

foregrounds, landscapes,
    107-8
foreshortening, 49
form, 42-3
frottage, 17

G
Gould, Ted, 8, 9, 11, 51
grounds: textured, 98-9
 tinted, 88

H
hard pastels, 76
Harden, Elisabeth, 12, 53,
    57
Harrison, Hazel, 102, 105
hatching, 16, 23, 30
highlights, lifting out, 19
horizon, 60-1
Horton, James, 51, 54-5

I
impressing, 31
inks, 15
 brush drawing, 26-7
 coloured, 29, 34-5
 pen and ink, 22-3

J
Jordan, Maureen, 71, 74,
    81, 115, 116, 123,
    125

K
Klee, Paul, 8

L
La Tour, Maurice Quentin de, 72, 80, 122
landscapes, 106-13
lifting out, 18-19
light and dark, 42-3
lightening pastels, 82
line drawings, 16, 24-5, 44-5, 80
Liotard, Jean-Etienne, 80
lost-and-found edges, 44
Lowe, Vicky, 57

M
Manifold, Debra, 102, 104
markers, 34
Marsters, Geoff, 72, 73, 84, 107, 122
Martin, Judy, 36-7, 56, 58-9, 75
Maxwell Wood, Robert, 9, 56, 123
measuring, 38-9, 49, 63
mixed media, 64-7
monochrome drawing materials, 14-15
monochrome techniques, 16-27
Moore, Elizabeth, 36-7, 74
movement, 50, 57

N
negative shapes, 41
nudes, 48-52

O
oil pastels, 29, 32, 36-7, 76, 92-3, 104
outline drawings, 40, 43
overlays, pastels, 85

P
Paine, Ken, 71, 122, 126-7
papers: for drawing, 15
  for pastels, 29, 32-3, 78-9, 84-9, 96-7
  stretching, 24-5
pastels, 29, 32-3, 36-7, 54-5, 70-127
pencils, 14, 16
  coloured, 28-9, 30-1, 36-7, 58-9
  pastel pencils, 32, 76
pens, 15, 22-3, 24
perspective, 11, 49, 60-2
photographs, 57
Picasso, Pablo, 22
portraits, 122-4, 126-7
Poussin, Nicolas, 24
proportion: buildings, 62-3
  figure drawing, 48-9
putty erasers, 19

R
Raney, Karen, 57, 64-7
Rembrandt, 24, 26
resist, wax, 34

S
sandpaper, 79, 96, 110-13
sanguine, 20, 21
Sansfix paper, 79, 96-7
Scott, Hil, 50
scribble drawing, 22
sgraffito, 32, 33, 100-1
shapes, 40-1
Sickert, Walter, 124
side strokes, pastels, 80-1
sight-size drawings, 38-9, 63
Simmonds, Jackie, 73, 74, 109, 115, 117
sketching, 46-7, 124
Strand, Sally, 124, 125
stretching paper, 24-5
Stubbs, George, 57

T
texture, papers, 18, 20, 78, 81
textured grounds, 98-9
tinted grounds, 88
tonal effects, 16, 43
Townend, John, 9, 12, 13, 46, 47, 62
trois couleurs, 21

U
underdrawings, 94-5, 122
underpainting, pastels, 90-1

V
vanishing point, 60-2

W
washes, 24-5, 88
wax resist, 34
wet brushing, 89, 92-3
white line drawing, 31
white spirit, 104

Stockists & Suppliers

Australia and New Zealand

ACT Paper Pty Ltd
10 McGlore Street
Micham
Victoria 3132

E & F Good
31 Landsdowne Terrace
Walkerville SA 5081

Kaori Art and Craft Centre
264 Karon Road
Kaori
New Zealand

United Kingdom

Binney & Smith
 (Liquitex UK)
Ampthill Road
Bedford MK42 9RS

Cornelissen & Son Ltd
105 Great Russell Street
London WC1B 3RY

Daler-Rowney Ltd
PO Box 10
Southern Industrial Estate
Bracknell
Berkshire RG12 8ST

John Mathieson & Co.
48 Frederick Street
Edinburgh EH2 1HG

Russell & Chapple Ltd
Canvas & Art Materials
23 Monmouth Street
London WC2H 9DE

Winsor & Newton
Whitefriars Avenue
Wealdstone, Harrow
Middlesex HA3 5RH

United States

Art Supply Warehouse
360 Main Avenue
Norwalk, CT 06851
(mail order)

Binney & Smith Artist'
 Materials
1100 Church Lane
PO Box 431
Easton, PA 18042

Boncour Artist's Colors Inc.
Zipatone Inc.
150 Fence Lane
Hillside, IL 60162

Chromacryl (Australia)
US Distributor
Chrome Acrylics
40 Tanner Street
Haddonfield, NJ 08033

Daniel Smith Inc.
Fine Arts Materials
4130 First Avenue South
Seattle, WA 98134

NY Central Art Supply
62 Third Avenue
New York, NY 10003

Pearl Paint Corporation
308 Canal Street
New York, NY 10013

Standard Brands Paint
 Company
4300 West 190th Street
Torrance, CA 90509-2956

Utrecht Manufacturing
 Corporation
33 35th Street
Brooklyn, NY 11232

Winsor & Newton, Inc.
US Office
11 Commission Avenue
PO Box 1396
Piscataway, NJ 08033

Notes

NOTES

NOTES

NOTES

DRAWING WITH
PENCILS
PASTELS

DRAWING WITH
PENCILS
& PASTELS

HAZEL HARRISON

SELECT
EDITIONS

Select Editions imprint specially produced for Selectabook Limited

© Anness Publishing Limited 1996, 1999, 2000, 2002

Produced by Anness Publishing Limited
Hermes House
88–89 Blackfriars Road
London SE1 8HA

ISBN 1 84038 807 2

A CIP catalogue record for this book is available from the British Library

Publisher: Joanna Lorenz
Project Editor: Samantha Gray
Designer: Michael Morey
Photographers: Paul Forrester, John Freeman
Production Controller: Don Campaniello

Previously published as part of a larger compendium, *How to Paint and Draw*

Printed and bound in China

1 3 5 7 9 10 8 6 4 2